Healing from Jesus

Peter Scothern

New Wine Press

New Wine Press
PO Box 17
Chichester
PO20 6YB
England

First published by New Wine Press in 1985

Bible references are from the Authorised Version.

ISBN 0 947852 10 7

Typeset by CRB Associates, Reepham, Norfolk.
Printed in England by Clays Ltd, St Ives plc.

Contents

Preface

Although the ministry of divine healing is now much more accepted, it has required a pioneer work over the years. For the last 50 years Peter Scothern has been used by God in this ministry, visiting numerous countries and seeing the hand of the Lord at work.

He has ministered in all denominations and been involved in community revivals in West Wales, the Midlands and Essex. Abroad he has visited the USA, Europe, Africa and India where over 75,000 have attended his outdoor miracle crusades.

Thousands have come to Christ through his simple but powerful gospel ministry, and he has witnessed hundreds of miracles of healing – the deaf, dumb, blind, lame, cancer victims and every sort of sickness.

This book is intended to build up your faith to receive any healing you may need, or to help someone sick.

May the Lord speak to you through it.

Dedicated to Natalie Pearson who faithfully served this ministry for over forty years and assisted with the preparation of this text.

Chapter 1

Those Vital Questions

For over 50 years I have been involved in the ministry of divine healing. During this period I have witnessed many remarkable cures and received numerous enquiries on the subject of divine healing. I render praise and glory to Jesus for being called of God to such a Christ-exalting ministry, and for the numerous manifestations of His healing grace and power that I have been privileged to witness. My in-depth experience has revealed there are two basic questions frequently asked by those seeking divine healing.

First, why are we sick? That is the cause, the reason, the origin of our sickness. Second, how can God heal us? That is the remedy, the means, the process by which the Lord heals. These basic questions will always remain in our thoughts as we peruse the contents of this book. Certainly they should be prevalent in the mind of the committed Christian who is sincerely seeking the blessing of divine healing.

An additional purpose of this study is to provide simple scriptural answers to such questions as, 'What is divine healing?' 'Is divine healing in the Atonement?' 'Is it God's will to heal?' 'Why are some not healed?' 'How should we pray for divine healing?'

'How much faith do we need?' 'What connection has Satan and his evil spirits with disease and sickness?' 'Can we claim divine health as well as divine healing?' For the answer to these vital questions we will turn to the Scriptures sincerely acknowledging *'all scripture is given by inspiration of God'*.

First we will consider how sickness and disease originated. This is indeed an intriguing and interesting issue. Using the Bible as our textbook let us refer to the first book in the Bible, Genesis 1:31:

> *'And God saw every thing that he had made, and, behold, it was very good. And the evening and the morning were the sixth day.'*

A careful examination of this text will enable us to consider the lead question, 'Where did sickness come from?' Notice everything that God created was very good, and certainly original man was included in this category. In fact the earlier verse of Genesis 1:27 confirms this:

> *'So God created man in his own image, in the image of God he created him; male and female he created them.'*

So the first man, Adam, was created in the image of God, and the Bible states *'he was very good'*. Without question this would exclude every evidence of sin or sickness. God's first man, Adam, was created sound and well, whole and healthy after God's divine image and divine order. Now turn to another enlightening passage of Scripture to be found in Genesis 2:15–17:

> *'And the Lord God took the man, and put him into the garden of Eden to dress it and to keep it. And the Lord God commanded the man, saying, Of every*

tree of the garden thou mayest freely eat: but of the tree of the knowledge of good and evil, thou shalt not eat of it: for in the day that thou eatest thereof thou shalt surely die.'

Adam disobeyed the Lord. The consequences were devastating. These are highlighted in the first statement made after Adam's transgression.

Genesis 3:9–10 reads:

'And the Lord God called unto Adam and said unto him, Where art thou?' And he said, I heard thy voice in the garden, and I was afraid, because I was naked; and I hid myself.'

Let us consider Adam's threefold confession.

1. *'I was afraid.'* The reality of sin and fear suddenly overtook Adam.
2. *'I was naked.'* This is an interesting statement. It has been suggested that Adam at his creation was clothed from within with the glory of God, while the animals were clothed without by skins and fur. The moment Adam severed fellowship with God, the glory of the Lord departed leaving Adam both spiritually and physically naked.
3. *'I hid myself.'* Adam's sin caused him to hide away from his holy creator revealing Adam's sin-consciousness and feeling of condemnation. The overall consequence of Adam's sin, however, was summed up in the Lord God's divine warning, *'for in the day that thou eatest thereof thou shalt surely die'.*

Now what was God saying? Again, the Scriptures reveal that as a direct result of Adam's sin, the law of sin began to affect the entire human race:

'Wherefore, as by one man sin entered into the world, and death by sin; and so death passed upon all men, for that all have sinned.'   (Romans 5:12)

'For if by one man's offence death reigned by one; much more they which receive abundance of grace and of the gift of righteousness shall reign in life by one, Jesus Christ. Therefore as by the offence of one judgement came upon all men to condemnation; even so by the righteousness of one the free gift came upon all men unto justification of life. For as by one man's disobedience many were made sinners, so by the obedience of one shall many be made righteous.'   (Romans 5:17–19)

The consequence of Adam's transgression meant the entire human race becoming contaminated by the law of sin accompanied by the devastating effects of the law of death. Now the law of death operated in two spheres of Adam's being. First, in the realm of the spirit when Adam was instantly separated from fellowship with God; secondly, in the realm of the physical when the law of death began to gradually and progressively take command. Adam did not die physically at this point in time; in fact he lived another 930 years. However, the Lord clearly stated, *'for in the day that thou eatest thereof thou shalt surely die'*.

The inference here in the original text is as follows: 'In dying thou shalt die', suggesting a process rather than an immediate physical death. We are informed that we begin to age, i.e. die progressively, from the time we are born. The process of growing old is a slow and certain death. Of course, sickness may accelerate this process. Without question, ageing is one of the major contributory factors to sickness and disease.

Once the body cells, muscles and nerves, etc. begin to deteriorate they become vulnerable to disease. Although growing old may be defined as a natural process, we must never forget that original ageing occurred as a direct consequence of Adam's initial transgression.

The twin evils of the law of sin and death were injected into the human race through the first act of sin. These destructive laws are powerful and devastating, promoting many of our calamities, miseries and illnesses.

However, as we proceed with this intriguing study we will discover to our great joy such verses as Romans 8:1–2:

> *'There is therefore now no condemnation to them which are in Christ Jesus, who walk not after the flesh, but after the Spirit. For the law of the Spirit of life in Christ Jesus hath made me free from the law of sin and death.'*

The violation of God's holy commandments continues to be one of the main causes of sickness throughout the Bible. We shall study some of these scriptures in turn.

Such instances as when Abimelech and his household suffered because they ignorantly disregarded God's holy laws. Later when the Lord raises up the nation of Israel He offers His services as their great Physician on the strict conditions that they comply with His divine commandments. Many other instances in Scripture clearly reveal the definite link between man's disobedience and the scourge of sickness and disease. This unquestionable scriptural connection between sin and sickness falls into two categories.

Adam's original fall is generally attributed to be the main cause of sickness and disease, although sickness may result from other exceptional causes. One classical example is to be found in Mark 2:5 where we read that four men brought a paralytic friend on a bed to Jesus. They experienced great difficulty in bringing the sick man into the immediate presence of the Lord because the house was crowded, so they contrived to get on to the roof and lower the sick man in the presence of Jesus on a stretcher. Jesus seeing the sick of the palsy said to him, *'Son, thy sins be forgiven thee.'*

Jesus obviously perceived that this man was beset with sin. Therefore, it was imperative that he first received the forgiveness of sins before the Lord could heal him. In fact the Psalmist also affirms that if we regard iniquity in our hearts the Lord will not hear us, Psalm 66:18. We must get our priorities right! We must receive the forgiveness of our sins before we ask for the healing of our bodies. This is the divine order. As soon as the palsied man received the forgiveness of sins our Lord was able to say to him, *'Arise, and take up thy bed, and go thy way into thine house.'* Immediately the man stood up and walked, glorifying the name of Jesus. This incident reveals the unquestionable connection between personal sin and sickness and disease. We will consider this in greater detail later.

Let us now look at some of the other causes of sickness and disease. Sickness may result from breaking natural laws. When God created the human body He produced natural laws to govern its growth and development. If we ignore these laws we will suffer. For example, if a man falls from a roof he may break his bones. If he does not eat he will ultimately starve. If he puts acid on his skin he will burn. There are natural codes of health which must be strictly observed. This is basic common sense. Let us consider a further matter of great importance. Supposing we drink alcohol excessively we will damage the tissues of our stomach. Supposing we inhale nicotine regularly we may permit cancerous cells to develop in our lungs resulting in serious illness. If we desire divine healing we must first ask God to deliver us from any such harmful habits. There is little point in asking God for divine healing if we continue to abuse and injure our bodies.

Now let us consider the effects of the breaking of God's commandments, e.g. the Sabbath. There are some who labour seven days a week intending to prosper and build up their bank balance but at the same time sacrificing their health. As time passes they continue to break God's sabbatical law until eventually it takes its toll in sickness, broken marriages or nervous breakdowns. God is not at fault – we are to blame for ignoring the sabbatical laws. Remember the Sabbath was made for man because God knew that we needed at least one day a week to rest, to worship, to refresh and rejuvenate ourselves spiritually and physically. So if we continually break God's sabbatical law we will do ourselves personal harm and sickness can result. So we must make absolutely sure that we are living and eating wisely, and taking proper rest.

Chapter 2

Disease May Be Caused
by Infirm Spirits

Sickness and disease may be caused by Satan and his spirits of infirmity. Once the devastating laws of sin and death had enslaved the human race man became vulnerable to Satan and his works. After all, it was Satan who sponsored the original act of rebellion in the garden of Eden. He master-minded Adam's original transgression. First, Satan seduced the serpent, who then in turn seduced Eve and finally Adam succumbed. Until this point Adam was no doubt adequately protected from sin and sickness. His close relationship with God ensured this. But once this relationship was broken Adam was vulnerable to the evils of Satan. Although there is no specific mention of sickness or disease during Adam's lifetime, nevertheless he became a victim of the laws of the sin and death. These destructive laws opened the doors to disease and sickness and afforded Satan the opportunity to use spirits of infirmity to accelerate his evil intentions.

Now, a simple study of the New Testament will clearly reveal that Jesus dealt with two categories of disease, those of 'natural' origin and those of 'spirit' origin. The following scriptures clarify this:

'And [Jesus] was teaching in one of the synagogues on the sabbath. And, behold, there was a woman which had a spirit of infirmity eighteen years, and was bowed together, and could in no wise lift up herself'. [I might suggest that she was suffering from an arthritic condition.] *'And when Jesus saw her, he called her to him, and said unto her, Woman, thou art loosed from thine infirmity. And he laid his hands on her: and immediately she was made straight, and glorified God.'*

(Luke 13:10–13)

Notice the two distinct ministries, first Jesus expelled the spirit of infirmity and then He laid His hands on her to complete the healing.

'And the ruler of the synagogue answered with indignation, because that Jesus had healed on the sabbath day, and said unto the people, There are six days in which men ought to work: in them therefore come and be healed, and not on the sabbath day. The Lord then answered him, and said, Thou hypocrite doth not each one of you on the sabbath loose his ox or his ass from the stall, and lead him away to watering? And ought not this woman, being a daughter of Abraham, whom Satan hath bound, lo, these eighteen years, be loosed from this bond on the sabbath day?. And when he had said these things, all his adversaries were ashamed: and all the people rejoiced for all the glorious things that were done by him.' (Luke 13:14–17)

Jesus confirmed that this sick woman was a victim of Satan's spirit of infirmity, i.e. a spirit-based evil which attacked her body. It is interesting to note that she possessed an Abraham-type faith and Jesus

Himself commended her spiritually; nevertheless her body became the target of the spirit of infirmity.

It is possible for God's children who are advanced in the faith to be attacked by a spirit of infirmity. This is not to be confused with demon possession. A demon is an evil spirit with an unclean nature which generally attacks the spirit or mind of a person. This, however, was a 'spirit of infirmity' whose chief ambition was to attack and destroy the body. Let me explain!

When a destructive germ life is basically responsible for our disease then we know an enemy is at work. The evil life in the germ or virus is bent upon the destruction of our health by attacking us. There are many scriptures to verify this.

In Matthew 12:22–23 we read:

> *'Then was brought unto* [Jesus] *one possessed with a devil, blind, and dumb: and he healed him, insomuch that the blind and dumb both spake and saw. And all the people were amazed and said, Is not this the son of David?'*

Now these verses state that the blindness and the dumbness were caused by a 'spirit of infirmity'. The man was also possessed with an unclean spirit but it was the spirits of infirmity which caused him to be blind and dumb. When Jesus cast them out the blind were able to see and the dumb to speak. Another interesting case is mentioned in Luke 4 where Jesus went to visit Simon's wife's mother who was taken with a great fever. Notice how Jesus stood over her and **rebuked** the fever. Immediately it departed from her and she arose and ministered unto them. It is illogical to rebuke an inanimate object, so obviously Jesus recognised that He was rebuking a **living thing**.

No doubt this was the spirit of infirmity which attacked Simon's wife's mother. Jesus rebuked it and expelled it. Then she arose and ministered unto them.

Notice also Luke 4:40–41:

> *'Now when the sun was setting, all they that had any sick with divers diseases brought them unto* [Jesus]; *and he laid his hands on every one of them, and healed them. And devils also came out of many, crying out, and saying, Thou art Christ the Son of God. And he rebuking them suffered them not to speak: for they knew he was the Christ.'*

The verb 'to rebuke' appears again in these verses. Jesus would **rebuke** a spirit of infirmity or **rebuke** a devil, expelling it with His authority and power.

It was the destructive life-force of the disease that Jesus exorcised when He healed the sick. We all grew from a tiny germ; the life-force of that germ originated with God. Now as long as the natural life remains the body lives, but the moment the life departs the body dies. So it is with disease. As long as the destructive life of the germ or virus remains then the body continues to be diseased, but the moment the destructive life of the disease is expelled the offending disease becomes inactive. At this point the healing process begins. Jesus described such destructive diseases as 'spirits of infirmity'. He rebuked them and cast them out with unwavering authority.

How wonderful to know that the authority and the power of the Lord Jesus is invested in His name. In the name of Jesus the committed child of God is able to rebuke sickness and disease. Satan and sickness will hold no dominion over us if we believe that in the name of Jesus we have Christ's delegated power and authority. When we receive the Lord Jesus we also receive His imparted authority to resist every evidence of sin and sickness. Every spirit of infirmity is subject to the almighty name of Jesus.

Jesus declared after His resurrection:

'All power is given unto me in heaven and in earth.'
(Matthew 28:18)

That power and authority is invested in His name. When we take up the name of Jesus and resist the enemy he will surely flee from us (James 4:7).

Chapter 3

Divine Healing and the Passover Lamb

One of the less appreciated divine healing events concerns the 'Passover Lamb'. Exodus chapter 12 records the amazing story of the Lord's unprecedented deliverance of the Children of Israel from the mud camps of Egypt. The Hebrew slaves were instructed by the Lord's servant Moses to take an unblemished lamb of the first year and sacrifice it on the fourteenth day of the month. The blood was carefully caught in a basin and sprinkled with a hyssop upon the lintel and the doorpost of their houses. At midnight the death angel appeared to smite the first-born of man and beast, but the Israelites took refuge behind the blood-stained doors and were miraculously preserved. This event became known as 'the Passover' and continues to be celebrated by religious Jews unto this day.

Consider this remarkable Old Testament incident more carefully. First, the lamb that was chosen was without spot and blemish, a male of the first year. This is the first Old Testament type which unmistakably points to our Lord Jesus Christ, the coming Passover Lamb of God. The Lord Jesus was later crucified shedding His precious blood to save us from sin. This is the most important aspect of this event, and we give thanks to God for Jesus who was nailed to the cross, shedding His blood to save us all. However, we must personally apply the blood of the Lord Jesus to our hearts by faith before we can experience the real joy and assurance of our salvation. It is not sufficient to say that the Lamb of God died to take away the sin of the whole world. It is not sufficient simply to believe that Jesus the Lamb of God actually existed. We must sincerely repent and apply the precious blood of Jesus by faith to our hearts.

Also there is another important aspect of this event which is generally overlooked. After the Passover lamb was sacrificed and the blood sprinkled, the body of the lamb was roasted with fire and eaten.

> *'And they shall eat the flesh in that night, roast with fire, and unleavened bread; and with bitter herbs they shall eat it. Eat not of it raw, nor sodden at all with water, but roast with fire; his head with his legs, and with the purtenance thereof. And ye shall let nothing of it remain until the morning; and that which remaineth of it until the morning ye shall burn with fire.'* (Exodus 12:8–10)

An interesting cross-reference to this unique event is to be found in Psalm 105:37:

> *'He brought them forth also with silver and gold: and there was not one feeble person among their tribes.'*

As we examine this text carefully we will discover that when the Lord delivered the children of Israel from the land of Egypt He also made them **strong and well**. Notice the final phrase of this verse, *'there* *was not one feeble person among their tribes'*. How wonderful! The children of Israel who had suffered greatly under the harsh whip of their taskmasters were given divine healing and health before they set forth on their journey to the promised land. The scriptures suggest that through eating the body of the pascal lamb the children of Israel were provided with new health and healing.

Therefore a careful understanding of the Passover lamb incident reveals a twofold blessing. First, the Israelites were delivered from certain death by the sprinkling of blood. Secondly, they were divinely healed and strengthened by eating the body of the lamb.

Now these two basic blessings are present in the Holy Communion service, in the form of two emblems, namely the bread and the wine. The bread is symbolic of the body of our Lord Jesus Christ, while the wine speaks of His precious blood. These two symbols betoken the twin blessings of the New Covenant secured for us by our Lord Jesus, i.e. the forgiveness of our sins and the divine healing of our mortal bodies. How wonderful it would be if every dedicated minister and priest would teach these two basic truths when celebrating the Holy Communion.

The apostle Paul declares:

> *'...not discerning the Lord's body. For this cause many are weak and sickly among you...'*
>
> (1 Corinthians 11:29–30)

When we clearly discern the body of our Saviour we sincerely recognise that He was scourged for our sicknesses and that with His stripes we are healed according to 1 Peter 2:24. As we partake of the bread which is the emblem of His body we should accept by faith the divine healing and strength which our Lord has provided.

Also remember that our Lord Jesus Christ is now glorified and seated at the right hand of the Majesty on high. The bread therefore can betoken His **glorified** person suggesting we also receive strength and life and power from our risen Lord now seated in the heavenlies.

The Bible calls **this** life 'eternal life', meaning the very life nature of God Himself in the person of our Lord Jesus Christ. So as the bread betokens the body of our Saviour the wine also betokens the blood of our Lord Jesus. His precious blood was shed for sinners and the Bible promises that if we confess our sin He is faithful and just to forgive and to cleanse us from all unrighteousness (1 John 1:9). This simply means that each time we take the cup and drink the wine at the communion service we may positively claim the forgiveness of all our sins, and each time we take the bread we may positively claim the healing of all our diseases. There is forgiveness and healing at the Lord's Table which is a fulfilment of the Passover provisions in the book of Exodus.

Let us now consider the healing sign given to Moses. For in the Exodus chapter 3 the angel of the Lord appeared unto Moses in a flame of fire from a burning bush which was not consumed.

And Moses said, I will now turn aside, and see this great sight, why the bush is not burnt. And when the LORD *saw that he turned aside to see, God called unto him out of the midst of the bush, and said, Moses, Moses. And he said, Here am I. And [God] said, Draw not nigh hither: put off thy shoes from off thy feet, for the place whereon thou standest is* *holy ground. Moreover he said, I **am** the God of thy father, the God of Abraham, the God of Isaac, and the God of Jacob. And Moses hid his face.'*

(Exodus 3:3–6)

The Lord revealed unto Moses that he was to be the chosen vessel to bring deliverance to the children of Israel.

'Now therefore, behold, the cry of the children of Israel is come unto me: and I have also seen the oppression wherewith the Egyptians oppress them. Come now therefore, and I will send thee unto Pharaoh, that thou mayest bring forth my people the children of Israel out of Egypt.'   (Exodus 3:9–10)

When Moses faced up to this tremendous responsibility he pleaded his natural weaknesses.

'And Moses answered and said, But, behold, they will not believe me, nor hearken unto my voice: for they will say, The Lord has not appeared unto thee.'

(Exodus 4:1)

The Lord counteracted Moses' deficiencies by furnishing him with the supernatural evidence of His divine appointment. In Exodus 4:2–8 we read that one of the signs God gave to Moses was that he temporarily became a leper, and later God supernaturally healed him. Leprosy was a dreaded curse in those days. Leperous victims were ostracised from society, often succumbing to this cruel wasting disease. For Moses to appear one moment a leper and the next miraculously cured was indeed an amazing sign. No doubt this was intended to prove the sovereign authority of the Lord God to both afflict in judgement and to heal in mercy.

21

A classic example is to be found in Numbers 12. Divine judgement befell Miriam when she became involved in a gossip crusade against Moses. She had criticized Moses because he had married an Ethiopian woman (Numbers 12:1). The Lord certainly frowned upon Miriam's cruel criticism and plagued her with leprosy. She had touched the Lord's anointed, a certain warning to all of God's people. I often wonder how many of the Lord's children succumb to sickness because they have participated in some gossip crusade and like Miriam became involved with scandal, criticism, back-biting etc. Miriam was one of Israel's leading women and should have known better.

Maybe the apostle James had this in mind when he suggested:

> *'Confess your faults one to another, and pray for one another, that ye may be healed. The effectual fervent prayer of a righteous man availeth much.'*
>
> (James 5:16)

This sobering incident emphasizes the need for us to examine ourselves before the Lord in case this has a bearing upon the vital question, 'Why am I sick?'

However, this incident concludes on a satisfactory note as Miriam sincerely repented and Moses called upon the name of the Lord on her behalf.

Next we will consider God's great covenant of healing, from Exodus 15:26, Jehovah Rapha, *'I am the Lord that healeth thee'*.

This divine promise was given to the children of Israel as they journeyed through the burning desert towards Canaan. They were subject to ravaging elements, the blistering sun and every natural discomfort, but here the Lord God assured His people *'I **am** the* LORD *that healeth thee'*. This sacred healing covenant, however, was strictly geared to pre-determined conditions.

> *'So Moses brought Israel from the Red sea, and they went out into the wilderness of Shur; and they went three days in the wilderness, and found no water. And when they came to Marah, they could not drink of the waters of Marah, for they were bitter: therefore the name of it was called Marah. And the people murmured against Moses, saying, What shall we drink? And he cried unto the* LORD; *and the* LORD *shewed him a tree, which when he had cast into the waters, the waters were made sweet: there he made for them a statute and an ordinance, and there he proved them and said, If thou wilt diligently hearken to the voice of the* LORD *thy God, and wilt do that which is right in his sight, and wilt give ear to his commandments, and keep all his statutes, I will put none of these diseases upon thee, which I have brought upon the Egyptians: for I **am** the* LORD *that healeth thee.'*
> (Exodus 15:22–26)

Implicit obedience to God's commandments linked with a continuing desire to do His will are obviously basic conditions for divine healing. It is interesting to note that the covenant also provides for God to protect His people from disease. This truth is also confirmed in Psalm 91:10:

> *'There shall no evil befall thee, neither shall any plague come nigh thy dwelling.'*

A more detailed understanding of God's healing covenant may inspire and enlighten the reader.

Jehovah Rapha

*'I **am** the* Lord *that healeth thee.'*   (Exodus 15:26)

First let us consider the pronoun 'I'. '**I**' am the Lord that healeth thee. The Almighty God, the Omnipotent One, the Maker of heaven and earth, the creator of all things, the supreme Lord of the universe, the Father of our Lord Jesus Christ, the God of Abraham, Isaac and Jacob promises to be our healer and physician. If we observe His commandments He solemnly promises to take upon Himself the responsibility of our divine doctor and physician. Now supposing we purchase an item which carries a guarantee and after a few weeks that item ceases to function correctly. There are generally two options available. We may take the item either to a repairer or to the manufacturer. The manufacturer undoubtedly would prove the most ideal because he created the item in the first place. He is perfectly acquainted with every detail of its function and performance. The Lord Himself created us and He is therefore completely capable of putting us right.

Secondly, let us consider the divine title '**I AM**', I AM the Lord that healeth thee. This clearly emphasizes, the ever-present presence of the eternal God. Notice the tense, 'I AM', always present tense, i.e. '**In the *now***'. Some may argue that this covenant promise of healing in Exodus 15:26 belongs exclusively to the children of Israel. This is not so! The very name 'I AM' projects the living God into 'the now'. God is assuredly revealing that His divine surgery is always open, that He is always ready to bless and heal.

Let us consider the third section, I am '**the Lord**' that healeth thee. The God of creation is truly **the**

Lord. There is nothing too hard for Him. Jesus is the unquestionable Master of all diseases, sickness and affliction. All things are possible to Him who is enthroned in the heavens. No sickness, plague or disease can ignore His authority. Every knee must bow before the King of kings and the Lord of lords. His authority is supreme! He is the omnipotent One, the all powerful Lord and Master of the universe. He can heal all manner of sickness and disease. There is no affliction He cannot cure, because He is truly the Lord.

Now let us consider the next two words, I am the Lord **'that *healeth*'** thee. The verb 'to heal' means to recover, to recuperate, to make well again. This suggests a process rather than an instant cure. It is also present tense, a sure and certain declaration of God's willingness to heal us in the 'now'. I am the Lord **that healeth**. Praise God! He is still in the healing ministry today.

Finally, consider the last word of this covenant promise, I am the Lord that healeth **'thee'**. Oh! the wonder of it all! The Great Physician reveals a compassionate interest in the individual. Granted, this covenant promise was delivered to an entire nation but nevertheless it was the birthright of every individual who would observe its conditions.

A Brethren lady lay dying in a hospital ward. As she meditated on the Scriptures her attention focused on 1 Peter 2:24:

> *'Who His own self bare our sins in his own body on the tree, that we, being dead to sins, should live unto righteousness: by whose stripes ye were healed.'*

She considered the first section of the verse visualising how Jesus had died upon the cross to save her soul from sin. Then her thoughts centred upon the latter part of the verse: *'by whose stripes ye were healed'*. At first, she failed to understand the specific meaning of these remarkable words, when it suddenly dawned upon her that Jesus had not only died to save her lost soul but also to heal her sick body. She thought about the whip lacerations, the scourge marks inflicted on the body of Jesus by the cruel scourging. She understood how Jesus was striped to provide the blessing of divine healing.

'Nurse!' she cried, 'come quickly!'

The ward nurse hastened to her bed-side.

'Nurse!' she requested, 'please get my clothes. I am going home. I have just read in God's word that Jesus has healed me.'

The nurse was taken aback and called for the ward sister.

'Sister,' requested the patient again, 'please get my clothes, I am going home, I am healed.'

She was so persistent and determined that eventually she returned home. After a while her health was miraculously restored and she began testifying everywhere of the healing grace of the Lord Jesus Christ. It was her personal revelation and application of God's word that brought about this remarkable cure. God's concern for the individual is clearly expressed in His covenant promise of healing:

'I am the Lord that healeth thee.'

(Exodus 15:26)

Chapter 4

The Brazen Serpent Incident

Israel's historical journey to Canaan provides another unprecedented incident of Divine healing and deliverance:

> '*And they journeyed from mount Hor by the way of the Red sea, to compass the land of Edom: and the soul of the people was much discouraged because of the way. And the people spake against God, and against Moses, Wherefore have ye brought us up out of Egypt to die in the wilderness? for there is no bread, neither is there any water; and our soul loatheth this light bread. And the* LORD *sent fiery serpents among the people, and they bit the people; and much people of Israel died. Therefore the people came to Moses, and said, We have sinned, for we have spoken against the* LORD*, and against thee; pray unto the* LORD*, that he take away the serpents from us. And Moses prayed for the people. And the* LORD *said unto Moses, Make thee a fiery serpent, and set it upon a pole: and it shall come to pass, that everyone that is bitten, when he looketh upon it, shall live. And Moses made a serpent of brass, and put it upon a pole, and it came to pass, that if a*

Once again the children of Israel were in serious trouble. This time they indulged in a 'Complaint Campaign'. You would have thought they had learned their lesson from Miriam's bitter experience, but no, they complained bitterly against God and Moses forgetting the mighty victories Jehovah had recently granted them over the Canaanites.

How quickly we can lose sight of the faithfulness and goodness of God and become victims of self-inflicted discouragement and depression.

During this hazardous wilderness journey the Lord constantly preserved and protected His people from the oppressing natural elements. These included the poisonous snakes and serpents which lived in the desert.

When Israel launched her 'Complaints Campaign' the Lord withdrew His protecting hand and the poisonous serpents invaded the camp, many falling victim to their venom. Immediately there was great consternation and a cry of anguish. Once again, Moses consulted the Lord and received divine directions to bring a stop to this self-imposed tragedy.

A serpent of brass was raised on a wooden pole in the midst of the afflicted assembly. The victims who gazed on the uplifted serpent were miraculously saved, restored and healed. Jesus later used this event to reveal the true meaning of His own death upon the cross.

'And as Moses lifted up the serpent in the wilderness, even so must the Son of man be lifted up: That whosoever believeth in him should not perish, but have eternal life.' (John 3:14–15)

A more in-depth analysis of God's merciful blessings provided through the brazen serpent may be summed up as follows:

1. The Israelites were **granted forgiveness** from the abhorrent sin which they committed against God and His servant Moses.
2. They were **saved** from natural death.
3. They were **healed** from the lethal effect of the serpent bite – a type of divine healing. Once the snake poison entered the blood stream the victim would experience a slow agonizing death, but God in great mercy provided forgiveness and healing for all those who would accept His gracious provision.

The brazen serpent incident clearly reveals the twin mercies of redemption, i.e. forgiveness for the soul and the healing of the body. These twin mercies are the foundation stones of redemption. They are certainly the dual mercies of the new covenant. When our Lord Jesus was raised onto the cross His atoning death provided the twin redemptive blessings of forgiveness from all our sins and the healing of all our diseases.

> *'Who his own self bare our sins in his own body on the tree, that we, being dead to sins, should live unto righteousness: by whose stripes ye were healed.'*
>
> (1 Peter 2:24)

David the psalmist adds further confirmation to these twin blessings in Psalm 103:3:

> *'Who forgiveth all thine iniquities; who healeth all thy diseases.'*

A family emigrating to Australia prepared for their long journey. Among their provisions they took a food hamper containing cream crackers and cheese. Every time the passengers made their way to the dining room the family opened their food hamper and partook of their simple provision. They were convinced they could not afford the meal prices. After some days the young son complained bitterly about the monotony of the cream crackers and cheese. His parents eventually allowed him to visit the restaurant and enquire about the price of the food. An hour later he returned having enjoyed a scrumptious meal. His parents were angry and demanded to know how he had obtained the money to pay for the food. The boy replied 'I didn't pay for my lunch. It was included in the fare for our ticket.' His parents then realised that their fare to Australia included the price of all their meals.

There are many Christians who have yet to realise that Divine Healing is included in their 'ticket' of redemption. When Jesus redeemed the soul from sin He also redeemed the body from disease. **Divine healing is not an optional extra. It is one of the major benefits of our salvation.** It is rooted in the atoning work of our Lord Jesus Christ.

> *'That it might be fulfilled which was spoken by Esaias the prophet, saying, Himself took our infirmities, and bare our sicknesses.'*   (Matthew 8:17)

God does not intend us to bear the sickness Jesus has already borne. There would be no point in Jesus bearing our diseases if God intended us to bear them. Jesus bore our sins that we should be saved. Jesus also bore our sicknesses that we should be healed.

The brazen serpent incident unquestionably reveals the 'twin mercies' of **Christ's** redemption.

Chapter 5

The Complex Story of Job

Even a brief study of the Old Testament will reveal God's continuing concern for the sick and suffering. Almost every book in the Bible contains some incident where His healing grace and power is demonstrated.

We will now refer to the Book of Job.

Let us consider the main ingredient in this intriguing Old Testament drama. First we are introduced to the moral and spiritual attainments of Job the servant of God.

> 'There was a man in the land of Uz, whose name was Job; and that man was perfect and upright, and one that feared God, and eschewed evil.'   (Job 1:1)

Then we are told how the Lord and Satan became involved in Job's affairs.

> 'Now there was a day when the sons of God came to present themselves before the LORD, and Satan came also among them. And the LORD said unto Satan, Whence comest thou? Then Satan answered the LORD, and said, From going to and fro in the earth, and from walking up and down in it. And the LORD said unto Satan, Hast thou considered by servant

Job, that there is none like him in the earth, a perfect and upright man, one that feareth God, and escheweth evil? Then Satan answered the Lord, *and said, Doth Job fear God for nought? Hast not thou made a hedge about him, and about his house, and about all that he hath on every side? thou hast blessed the work of his hands, and his substance is increased in the land. But put forth thine hand now, and touch all that he hath, and he will curse thee to thy face. And the* Lord *said unto Satan, Behold, all that he hath is in thy power; only upon himself put not forth thine hand. So Satan went forth from the presence of the* Lord*.'* (Job 1:6–12)

Job's conflict intensified when God permitted Satan to afflict him with sore boils.

'And the Lord *said unto Satan, Behold, he is in thine hand; but save his life. So went Satan forth from the presence of the* Lord*, and smote Job with sore boils from the sole of his foot unto his crown. And he took him a potsherd to scrape himself withal; and he sat down among the ashes.'* (Job 2:6–8)

Although surrounded with negative attitudes Job's confidence in God remained steadfast.

'Then said his wife unto him, Dost thou still retain thine integrity? curse God, and die. But he said unto her, Thou speakest as one of the foolish women speaketh. What? shall we receive good at the hand of God, and shall we not receive evil? In all this did not Job sin with his lips.' (Job 2:9–10)

'Though he slay me, yet will I trust in him: but I will maintain mine own ways before him.' (Job 13:15)

*'For I know that my redeemer liveth, and that he
shall stand at the latter day upon the earth.'*
(Job 19:25)

Although mystified by these sinister events Job
sought to discover why he had been subject to such
a devastating onslaught. The truth is eventually
revealed. A secret fear had festered in Job's mind
demolishing the hedge which surrounded him.

*'Now a thing was secretly brought to me, and mine
ear received a little thereof. In thoughts from the
visions of the night, when deep sleep falleth on men,
fear came upon me, and trembling, which made all
my bones to shake.'* (Job 4:12–14)

So the complexities of Job's experience are clearly
revealed.

First, Satan conspired to attack Job, probably
because he was a righteous man. The righteous are a
continual target for Satan's relentless opposition.

Secondly, Job became vulnerable to Satan's attack
the moment he allowed fear to master his mind. Fear
always gives Satan a distinct advantage over us.

Thirdly, God permitted Satan to afflict Job to a
pre-determined degree and in the process exposed
Job's fear. Once Job acknowledged his fear with
repentance the Lord promptly put Satan to flight.
Righteous Job was forgiven, healed and fully
restored.

*'So the LORD blessed the latter end of Job more than
his beginning: for he had fourteen thousand sheep,
and six thousand camels, and a thousand yoke of
oxen, and a thousand she asses. He also had seven
sons and three daughters.'* (Job 42:12–13)

Finally, there is one other unique facet to this fascinating saga.

> *'And the* Lord *turned the captivity of Job, when he prayed for his friends: also the* Lord *gave Job twice as much as he had before.'* (Job 42:10)

Another aspect of Job's righteousness is revealed when he temporarily forgot his own predicament and began praying for others, a challenge indeed to all sufferers to pray for others less fortunate than themselves.

The Healing Prophets

Further evidence of God's healing love flows through the books of Kings. The most eminent prophets endowed with healing ministries were undoubtedly Elijah and Elisha.

Elijah the Tishbite was born in a small village named Tishbe, which in turn means 'Converter'. Truly it can be said that Elijah fervently dedicated his spiritual zeal to converting Israel from her rebellious ways. The prophet was frequently outlawed by King Ahab and Queen Jezebel. His life was under constant threat. The final show-down with the false prophets of Baal on Mount Carmel was a masterpiece of Jehovah's ingenuity coupled with Elijah's courage and determination to bring the nation back to God. Healing miracles were an added confirmation, although these were frequently manifest in private surroundings. Maybe the cleansing of the Syrian General Naaman was an exception.

Chapter 6

Naaman and
the Jordan Healing

At the height of his career Naaman, the captain of the host of the King of Syria, discovered he was a leper. This cruel wasting disease would ostracize him from society so the details were closely kept within his family circle. An Israeli servant girl employed by the Naaman household testified of Elisha's healing gifts. Arrangements were promptly made through diplomatic channels for Naaman to travel through Israel to visit the renowned prophet of God.

The events which followed are most enlightening. Naaman held rigid pre-conceived ideas as to how the prophet should heal him and reacted angrily when events took a different course.

> 'So Naaman came with his horses and with his chariot, and stood at the door of the house of Elisha. And Elisha sent a messenger unto him, saying, Go and wash in the Jordan seven times, and thy flesh shall come again to thee, and thou shalt be clean. But Naaman was wroth, and went away, and said, Behold, I thought, He will surely come out to me, and stand and call on the name of the LORD his God, and strike his hand over the place, and recover

the leper. Are not Abana and Pharpar, rivers of Damascus, better than all the waters of Israel? may I not wash in them, and be clean? So he turned and went away in a rage.'   (2 Kings 5:9–12)

Frequently those seeking divine healing tend to hold rigid ideas.

They remind me of a story about blind Bartimaeus. Before Jesus came on the scene at Jericho a friend asked the blind man how he expected Jesus to restore his sight. 'Oh,' replied Bartimaeus, 'He will send me to the Pool of Siloam to wash.'

Just because Jesus healed a blind man at the pool at Siloam it did not necessarily imply that Bartimaeus was to be healed in the same way. The Lord miraculously restored the sight of many blind persons in the New Testament, but He always cured them by different methods. So it is essential to keep an open attitude concerning the Lord's method to heal. In humility we must seek the will of God through the Scriptures, implicitly obeying His divine instruction. We may become victims of traditional ideas even in the realm of the Divine Healing Ministry.

Once Naaman had swallowed his pride and had listened to the wise counsel of a close servant he eventually condescended to wash seven times in the River Jordan. At this point another interesting question arises. Was Naaman progressively healed or did he have to wait until the final washing before he was cured?

The Scriptures do not furnish the answer to this intriguing question but an important issue is raised. Whichever way Naaman was cured it is important to remember that the verb 'to heal' suggests a process, rather than an instantaneous work of grace.

There is a clear indication in the Scriptures that the working of miracles and the gifts of healing are two distinct and separate manifestations of the Holy Spirit. Paul's epistle to the Corinthians confirms this:

'For to one is given by the Spirit the word of wisdom; to another the word of knowledge by the same Spirit; To another faith by the same Spirit; to another the gifts of healing by the same Spirit; To another the working of miracles; to another prophecy; to another discerning of spirits; to another divers kinds of tongues; to another the interpretation of tongues; But all these worketh that one and the selfsame Spirit, dividing to every man severally as he will.'
(1 Corinthians 12:8–11)

So the process of healing must not be confused with the working of miracles. This vital truth will help cushion the disappointment sometimes experienced by those who seek Divine Healing and fail to receive an immediate cure.

When Jesus healed the nobleman's son in John chapter 4 it distinctly states that he **began to amend** at the seventh hour.

'Jesus saith unto him, Go thy way; thy son liveth. And the man believed the word that Jesus had spoken unto him, and he went his way. And as he was now going down, his servants met him, and told him, saying, Thy son liveth. Then inquired he of them the hour when he began to amend. And they said unto him, Yesterday at the seventh hour the fever left him. So the father knew that it was at the same hour, in the which Jesus said unto him, Thy son liveth: and himself believed, and his whole house.'
(John 4:50–53)

There are a number of cases in the New Testament where testimony is given to the healing of the sick rather than the working of instant cures. Let it be stated once again that the true definition of healing is by process rather than by immediate deliverance. Naaman could have been cured either way. After all it is God's prerogative to work a miracle if He chooses. Our responsibility is to believe and obey.

Chapter 7

Discerning Our Lord's Body

The apostle Paul addressing the Christians at Corinth reminded them of their spiritual responsibilities before participating at the Lord's table. Before partaking of the bread and wine he exhorted them to carefully examine themselves and rectify any wrongs. Paul also adds:

> '...not discerning the Lord's body. For this cause many are weak and sickly among you...'
>
> (1 Corinthians 11:29–30)

What did the apostle mean, 'not discerning the Lord's body'?

A close examination of our Lord's body would have revealed the stripes He endured. These were the wounds inflicted by His tormentors prior to His crucifixion. These wounds are always associated with divine healing. These lacerations or stripes were received by our Lord Jesus in the judgement hall before He was crucified. The Roman soldiers, brandishing a whip, slashed the body of Jesus at least thirty-nine times. The whip comprised of long leather throngs containing acorn shaped leaded weights. This was applied with such brutal force and natural venom that many of the victims destined for crucifixion never reached the place of execution. They perished as a direct result of the indescribable horror of scourging. The prophet Isaiah having received a divine insight of this event prophesied:

> *'He is despised and rejected of men; a man of sorrows, and acquainted with grief: and we hid as it were our faces from him; he was despised, and we esteemed him not. Surely he hath borne our griefs, and carried our sorrows: yet we did esteem him stricken, smitten of God, and afflicted. But he was wounded for our transgressions, he was bruised for our iniquities: the chastisement of our peace was upon him; and with his stripes we are healed.'*
>
> (Isaiah 53:3–5)

The apostle Peter later reflecting upon the scourging of the Lord Jesus wrote after the event:

> *'Who his own self **bare our sins** in his own body on the tree, that we, being dead to sins, should live unto righteousness: by whose stripes **ye were** healed.'*
>
> (1 Peter 2:24)

Could this horrific ordeal to which Jesus willingly succumbed be the fulfilment of Matthew 8:17 – *'Himself took our infirmities, and bare our sicknesses'* – our diseases? Historical accounts of similar scourgings record how the victims received at least forty stripes, save one. Thirteen sickening lashes were laid upon each shoulder and thirteen across the broadest section of the back. Most victims lost both ears and eyes, and not a few were cruelly disembowelled resulting in a shocking death. Discerning our Lord's body helps us to perceive the deep scars caused by the cruel Roman whip. These sacred wounds are a perpetual reminder that divine healing has been purchased at a great price for all who will believe that our sickness and diseases were laid upon Jesus.

Another interpretation of discerning the Lord's body has a deeper spiritual meaning. It is proposed that the Lord's body comprises all Christian believers who are deemed to be members of His body. Not discerning or appreciating the oneness of believers may prove an obstacle to divine healing.

I recall an incident which took place during one of my crusade services. A local Christian businessman was a victim of arthritis. On many occasions he had sought divine healing without results. Eventually he became agitated and confused, and requested a personal interview. During our conversation the Lord revealed to me that he was holding something against another Christian. When I revealed this the sick man confessed that he deeply resented another Christian and had withheld the payment of certain debts. Acknowledging his sin before the Lord he promised to make immediate restitution. He promptly took out his cheque-book and made the necessary arrangements to pay the outstanding debt. Later that evening the Lord miraculously delivered him from every trace of arthritis.

Rightly discerning the Lord's body also involves maintaining a right relationship with the members of the Lord's body. As we forgive those who have trespassed against us so shall we be healed and forgiven. Not discerning the Lord's body may result in sickness and disease, but rightly discerning our Lord's body can result in being healed for the glory of God.

Chapter 8

The Heart of the Matter

The heart of the divine healing revelation certainly centres around the vital question: 'Did Jesus legally and in reality bear our sicknesses and our diseases?' Let us carefully examine the Scriptures as we consider this all important question.

Matthew 8:17 states:

> 'That it might be fulfilled which was spoken by Esaias the prophet saying, Himself took our infirmities and bare our sicknesses.'

The verb 'to bare' in this context is exactly the same as that found in 1 Peter 2:24:

> 'Who in his own self bare our sins in his own body on the tree, that we, being dead to sins, should live unto righteousness: by whose stripes ye were healed.'

'To bear' means to carry away, to remove. Jesus dealt with our sin problem by bearing our sins in His body on the cross. He legally carried away our sins. He became our sin-bearer. Those who believe this and willingly turn away from sin in sincere repentance take the initial step to salvation.

Jesus not only bore our sins, he also bore our sicknesses and diseases (Matthew 8:17). He legally carried them away. He became our sickness-bearer in exactly the same way He became our sin-bearer. The apostle Peter proclaims this irrefutable fact in the same verse of scripture: *'who in his own self bare our sins in his own body on the tree ... by whose stripes ye were healed'*. The very same Jesus, the holy Son of God who bore or sins, also bore our diseases. The word of God makes this absolutely clear.

Christ was scourged and striped for our healing; He was nailed to an old rugged cross to save us from our sins. As we accept these irrefutable facts we can receive both eternal life and divine healing. Divine healing like salvation is the birthright of every true child of God.

Divine healing is not an optional extra, it is a vital part of our total salvation. It is an all-inclusive salvation. After all, if Jesus had failed to redeem us from **all** the works of Satan we would need to look for another saviour to finish the incompleted work. But Jesus cried triumphantly from the cross, *'it is finished'*. He finished the work the Father gave Him to do and is now seated at the right hand of the Majesty on high. He has redeemed us from our sin and its consequences, and this includes sickness and disease.

Once the born-again child of God accepts this foundational truth he can lay positive claim to all redemptive blessings. As long as he subscribes to the conditions presented in the Word of God the child of the Lord has every right to all the redemptive blessings. Also having acknowledged that Jesus bore our sicknesses and diseases, it cannot be God's legal intention that we should bear them. God would not want us to bear what Jesus has already borne. Therefore, when God is able to exercise His perfect will in our lives He is more than willing to heal us. It is the enemy's delight to promote destructive diseases. God does not want His children to suffer from the works of Satan. Jesus came to destroy the works of the devil.

In Acts 10:38 we read:

'God anointed Jesus of Nazareth with the Holy Ghost and with power: who went about doing good, and healing all that were oppressed of the devil; for God was with him.'

Jesus declared war upon the works of Satan and overcame them triumphantly. Let us never forget that Jesus is the same yesterday, today and forever, and we can be certain that His attitude towards the works of Satan remain unchanged. Truly this is the heart of Divine Healing, that God has laid our sins and our diseases upon Jesus. He has provided a double cure for a double curse, i.e. forgiveness from **all** our sins and healing from **all** our diseases. Praise His holy Name.

Chapter 9

Divine Healing Is Our Inheritance

Divine Healing is our inheritance. We have a right to be well. Divine healing is our blood-bought right and provision. Jesus bequeathed health and healing to every child of God in His will and testament.

> '...by whose stripes ye were healed.' (1 Peter 2:24)

> '...Himself took our infirmities and bare our sicknesses.' (Matthew 8:17)

These positive promises point to an accomplished work. Jesus triumphantly cried from the cross, 'it is finished!' He successfully completed the work the Father gave Him to do. He bruised the head of Satan and triumphed over sin, sickness and even death. The victory of Jesus is the birthright of every child of God. His triumph is our triumph. His victory is our victory. He did nothing for Himself, He accomplished this on our behalf. He conquered sin, disease and sickness once and for all. He shares this mighty victory with all who will repent and believe on His name. Jesus bore our sins so that we might be saved. Jesus took our diseases so that we might be healed. He bore our infirmities, sicknesses and diseases so that we could claim full release and deliverance. We need not bear what Jesus has already borne.

This is the glorious message of the New Testament. We do not have to suffer if Jesus suffered for us. If we do suffer then we must discover why, and I am sure the Lord will reveal the reason and purpose. But one thing is sure, that God Himself will not lay upon us what He has already laid upon Jesus. Sickness and sin should not have dominion over us. We have the legal right to refuse every sickness and disease. Christ has redeemed us from all the works of Satan. Every sin, sickness and disease was credited to our Lord's account, He has borne them away by His triumphant death on the cross. Satan cannot legally lay upon us what God has laid upon Jesus. Satan has no right to afflict our bodies. We have every right to be free in the Name of Jesus. Divine healing is our inheritance, just as indeed salvation is our inheritance. Divine healing, like salvation, is our right and privilege.

Of course, it is left with each one of us to fulfil the terms of the divine conditions, in order to receive this marvellous provision. We can lay claim boldly to this redemptive grace; not with uncertainty, but with the confidence of positive faith. Jesus became our substitute for sin and sickness. That means He suffered for us, on our behalf.

A sympathiser is one who offers consolation. A sympathiser may prove helpful to the sufferer, but Jesus was more than a sympathiser. He actually became our substitute. He took our sins and our sickness so that we would not have to bear them. Sympathy may help us a little but what faith must recognise is that Jesus successfully carried away our sins and our sicknesses at Calvary. Because of this, healing is our inheritance. Divine healing has been successfully purchased by Christ's substitutionary death on the cross. We must recognise this tremendous truth. We must see our sickness, as well as our sins, laid upon the Lord Jesus. We do not have to bear them because Christ has already borne them. This blood-bought deliverance is the right of every child of God. Once we claim the promises we are set free.

Let me repeat, Jesus' victory was our victory, His triumph was our triumph. He did nothing for Himself, He did it all for us. In view of this irrefutable fact we must now take up the challenge.

The scripture says, *'ye are bought with a price'* (1 Corinthians 6:20), i.e. we are redeemed property.

We belong to the Lord Jesus Christ, we are no longer our own. We have been purchased by the redemptive grace of our Lord Jesus Christ, so Satan has no legal right to trespass upon our beings. We are within our rights to order Satan out of our lives and our bodies. In the Name of Jesus we can authoritatively exercise this right. We do this with the Word of God and not in our own strength or power. When our Lord was tempted in the wilderness He used the word of the Father to bring Satan to his knees. The usurper was smitten by the skilful use of the Word of God. We too must quote the Scriptures when we are under attack. We have a right to demand the restoration of our health in the Name of Jesus. We are no longer slaves of the devil. We are new creations in Christ Jesus once we have been truly saved by the grace of God. Therefore, we can rejoice in our blood-bought liberty and enjoy the health and healing that Jesus has provided. The Lord desires to bless and to heal us. He longs to make us sound and whole. This is the testimony that will glorify and praise His holy name. There is no doubt that God can give a limitless supply of grace to overcome all sickness and disease. Many have tested that through intense suffering they have been brought into a closer relationship with the Lord, but God receives even greater glory when we are able to testify of His miraculous healing power in our lives.

Consider the incident which took place at the gate of the Temple Beautiful in the the book of Acts chapter 3 when over five thousand souls a made commitment to Christ. This crippled man's miraculous healing brought great glory to God.

Recall the story of the Lord Jesus raising Lazarus from the dead in John chapter 11. Jesus made a remarkable statement in the early stages of this incident. He testified in verse 4, *'this sickness is not unto death, but for the glory of God, that the Son of God might be glorified thereby.'*

Lazarus eventually died, so what did Jesus mean when He said, *'this sickness is not unto death, but for the glory of God'*?

Our Lord knew that Lazarus would be raised from the dead. He foresaw the final resurrection miracle resulting in the glorification of His Father. It would seem that Jesus inferred that our sicknesses present us with an opportunity to trust God for our healing resulting in the glorification of His Name. This is precisely what happened in the case of Lazarus. After he was raised from the dead the name of the Lord was truly glorified. For we read in the Scriptures that after Lazarus was triumphantly raised from the dead many Jews believed on Him. I can recall hundreds of souls who have come to Christ after seeing our Lord's power healing the sick in my ministry. Full provision has been made for God's children to receive His divine blessing.

We must never, never surrender to temptation. We must never capitulate to sin. We must never surrender to sickness or disease. At the first sign or evidence we must stand resolutely upon the fact that Jesus has already dealt triumphantly with sin and sickness. Therefore, we have the legal right to order all disease out of our lives. We must resist disease exactly in the same way we resist sin. We must never allow Satan a bridgehead into our bodies. We must resist every symptom in the name of Jesus and continue to do so until we are fully and completely released. If the symptoms dare to return we must resist them again. We must resist in faith. We must command them to go in the name of the Lord.

We can resist the works of Satan in many ways, having been given this scriptural assurance in James 4:7, *'resist the devil, and he will flee from you.'* Sin and sickness are persistent these days. God's people everywhere are experiencing increasing opposition. We are in constant warfare with the power of darkness. On no account must we surrender to the enemy. We must not give an inch of ground to Satan, sin or sickness.

God instructs us as to how we can effectively resist the devil. First, we resist through **prayer**. Satan trembles when he sees the weakest saint upon his knees. Just to kneel before the Lord will frighten our enemy. As we sink down upon our knees and look into the face of our risen Lord, Satan will tremble. Prayer ground is overcoming ground. In prayer we can positively rebuke every advance of the enemy in the name of Jesus.

Secondly, we can resist through **praise**. Satan detests a praising saint. Shouts of praise brought down the walls of Jericho and threw open the prison doors at Philippi. We are exhorted to praise the Lord at all times. While we are praising the Lord, Satan has no room in our thoughts or conversation. Praise will scatter fear and gloom and put the enemy to flight. We must wear our garment of praise at all times, giving thanks to God for the victory which is ours through our Lord Jesus Christ.

Thirdly, we resist through **faith**. Remember we belong to the God of the universe. We are redeemed. We are His property. We are temples of the Holy Spirit. Satan has no right to trespass on God's property. We have every right in the name of Jesus to expel our enemy. We must confess that at all times we belong to the Lord. We must command sickness and disease to leave us. We must resist the devil and he will flee from us. We are not to be afraid, for in Christ we are complete. We are more than conquerors through Him that loved us. We must refuse to compromise. Our faith must always be positive and charged with Christ's authority.

Fourthly, we resist in the **name of Jesus**. Whenever we are tempted we must call upon the Name of the Lord. If prayer becomes difficult then simply repeat the name of Jesus over and over. Defy the devil in Jesus' name. Restrict his authority in the name of Jesus. Act your healing in the name of Jesus. Do all these things in the name of the Risen Lord. The phrase 'in the name of Jesus' simply implies 'in His stead' or 'as His ambassador'. Whatever we undertake in the name of Jesus simply means that we do this on His behalf. No nation would send forth an ambassador without giving that ambassador all the authority he required to conduct his business effectively. We take the name of Jesus with us wherever we go as ambassadors of the kingdom of God. In the name of Jesus the impossible becomes possible.

Fifthly, we resist through the **precious blood of Jesus**. If Satan attempts to bring up our past or even renew our symptoms we can defiantly confess '**the Blood of Jesus Christ, God's Son, has cleansed me from all sin**', or '**with His stripes we are healed**'. We must constantly remind the enemy of these devil-defeating truths. The precious blood of Jesus Christ is charged with **life** and **power**, and every mention of His blood enables us to draw on the very life-force of God Himself. We will effectively resist through the power that is in the blood of Jesus.

It is Satan's strategy to condemn and confuse us by reminding us of our past sins and failings. We must refuse these accusations. If we have sinned then we must promptly confess our sin, make restitution and then immediately claim the Lord's forgiveness. We must rise up and live righteously and positively for Jesus resisting every temptation and claiming forgiveness through the blood of Jesus.

Finally, we resist with the **promises of God**. The Word of God is the sword of the Spirit. It is an attacking weapon. Jesus successfully used the Word of God against Satan during the forty days of temptation in the wilderness. When Satan questioned Him, our Lord would reply again and again with the words, *'it is written'*. We must also take up the promises of God to resist sin and sickness and all the works of Satan. In the face of all opposition we must confess the Word of God. The Word of God is a sharp, two-edged sword and each time we say *'it is written'* we will put our infirmities to flight. As soldiers of the cross we must press through to ultimate victory. We must not allow one sin or sickness to molest us. We can effectively resist every sin, sickness and all demon power with the Word of God. Again and again, I exhort all who are experiencing severe testings from the enemy to resist with the Word of God. I have proved over many years during a time of prolonged conflict with the works of darkness that the Word of God has proved to be my ultimate weapon of victory. Christians under attack must use every spiritual weapon that God has made available, and then victory is certain. Resist the devil and he will flee from you! This is God's declaration and He will not break His word.

Chapter 10

How to Receive Divine Healing

There are various scriptural ways of receiving divine healing, but we must always remember that God Himself is the Divine Healer. If we accept this we can confidently take the following biblical instructions to receive God's healing.

The most practised method of divine healing is the 'laying on of hands' in the name of the Lord Jesus Christ. This instruction, given by the Lord Jesus, is found in Mark 16.

We read in verses 15–18:

> *'And He said unto them, Go ye into all the world, and preach the gospel to every creature. He that believeth and is baptised shall be saved; but he that believeth not shall be damned. And these signs shall follow them that believe; In my name shall they cast out devils; they shall speak with new tongues; they shall take up serpents; and if they drink any deadly thing, it shall not hurt them; they shall lay hands on the sick, and they shall recover.'*

Notice, Jesus said **'in my name ... they shall lay hands on the sick, and they shall recover,'** and Jesus Himself practised the ministry of the laying on of hands. Mark 16:17 states *'these signs shall follow them that believe'*, i.e. the believing ones. Christian believers have a right to minister the laying on of hands. Those who have believed on the Lord Jesus Christ as their Saviour may obey this instruction. The laying on of hands may be practised in a **private** capacity or in a **personal** sense, and it does not suggest that every believer is called or gifted to a **public ministry** of divine healing. But it certainly means that a Christian mother has a right to lay hands upon her sick child, or a believing husband has the right to pray for his sick wife. Sometimes when the laying on of hands is practised the patient may be overwhelmed by the Lord's power and presence. On one occasion I was ministering in an Anglican church when most of those seeking divine healing were overwhelmed. The local counsellors were on hand to assist with the ministry. When this experience occurs I remind those who have been so powerfully touched by the Lord that a concentration of God's power and blessing does not absolve us from our faith responsibilities. So after the sick folk are blessed in this unique way I encourage them to give thanks to God, and then rise up and act their faith while the anointing still rests upon them. During the last eventful crusade in Sierra Leone I encouraged the assisting pastors and ministers to help with the laying on of hands because there were so many requiring divine healing. I called the sick and afflicted forward according to their specific needs. First, I asked the lame and the crippled to assemble at the front where they lined up before the crusade platform. Then I instructed the local ministers and pastors to come forward and stand behind them. These dedicated men of God faithfully laid their hands upon the suffering in the name of the Lord Jesus. My responsibility was to pray a very powerful and authoritative prayer from the platform. As I began to pray, the Lord's healing grace and power came powerfully upon the sufferers, followed by a prolonged period of praise and thanksgiving. Then the pastors and clergy, under the inspiration of the Holy Spirit, began to encourage the sick to rise up and activate their faith in the name of the Lord. Within moments a profusion of healing and miracles took place which electrified the vast open-air assembly. We witnessed the lame throwing down their sticks and crutches and walking in the name of Jesus. The cripples began walking around, running and then jumping, praising and glorifying God. Those who were paralysed were seen walking, running and even jumping for joy. The amazing scenes which followed were certainly reminiscent of New Testament days.

The laying on of hands should be applied with as little physical pressure as possible. After all, it is simply a point of contact which releases the Lord's healing grace. An electric switch operates with little physical pressure, but the benefit is immediately effective. As the light fills the dark room with brilliance so the healing power of God will permeate the sick body. Laying on of hands is the point of contact which releases the healing grace of God. From that moment the sufferer must accept the immutability of God's promise and maintain an unwavering attitude of faith. The laying on of hands releases the Spirit of God to our sick and diseased minds and bodies. Once the power of the Lord surges through our sick beings then the divine life of our Lord Jesus brings supernatural healing.

Healing is a process, but with the help of the Holy Spirit, this process is accelerated. Sometimes a cure may take place in a moment of time, and this is classified as a miracle. Sometimes the healing may be progressive; this is classified as a healing. The verb 'to heal' in Mark 16 is linked with the verb 'to recover'. *'They shall lay hands on the sick, and they shall **recover'***, which means that they shall get better, suggesting a process rather than a miracle.

So the laying on of hands is our Lord's directive to *'them that believe'*. I remember proposing this on one occasion when I was lecturing on the ministry of divine healing. A young mother returned home to find that her child had taken sick. She felt it was right to call her doctor. The doctor came and certified that the child was sick, saying that he would call the next day having left her a prescription. She had to wait until her husband returned home from business before she could take the prescription down to the chemist. Then she recalled the message which I had given earlier about divine healing. She turned to Mark 16 and read the verses that I had outlined. *'These signs shall follow them that believe ... they shall lay hands on the sick, and they shall recover.'*

She spoke to the Lord saying, 'Lord Jesus, I believe on You and I am going to lay my hands upon my sick child in Your holy name. I believe You will keep Your word and heal my child'.

As the child was sleeping she gently laid her hands upon her child. Within an hour the temperature had subsided and the child made a wonderful recovery. The next morning when the doctor called, he was so pleased with her progress that he said there was no further need for him to call. This faithful Christian mother gave glory to God, for she knew in her heart that the healing power of Jesus had performed this wonderful thing.

The laying on of hands is simply a point of contact, assisting us to believe that at a specific moment God is healing us. Jesus said that when we pray we are to believe at that very moment that we have received what we ask for.

> *'Therefore I say unto you, What things soever ye desire, when ye pray, believe that ye receive them, and ye shall have them.'*   (Mark 11:24)

Notice that believing commences the moment we pray. When we pray and offer our prayer of healing to the Lord, we are to believe at that moment we have received what we asked for. That is the prayer of faith. The point of contact establishes both the time and place to expect God's divine healing. When we lay hands upon the sick we must believe at that moment the Spirit of the Living God will honour our obedience and quicken and heal according to the Lord's promise. From that moment we must believe in our hearts that God is already at work. There may not be any accompanying feeling or special sense experiences but we must trust the word and the promise of God without wavering. After the laying on of hands we must give praise and glory to God in simple faith, believing that the prayer has been heard and that God is already honouring His word in us.

The next scriptural divine healing instruction is to be found in James 5:14–15:

> *'Is any sick among you? let him call for the elders of the church; and let them pray over him, anointing him with oil in the name of the Lord: And the prayer*

of faith shall save the sick, and the Lord shall raise him up; and if he have committed sins, they shall be forgiven him.'

Note carefully there are three 'shalls' in this one promise: *'the prayer of faith **shall** save the sick', 'the Lord **shall** raise him up; and if he have committed sins, they **shall** be forgiven him'*. This means there are three blessings connected with one divine promise.

I would first like to draw your attention to the third of these blessings: *'if he have committed sins, they shall be forgiven him'*. It is imperative, of course, that the one seeking healing must be pure and clean from sin. In fact in verse 16, we are told, *'confess your faults to one another, and pray one for another, that ye may be healed'*. It is vital to recognise that if we are expecting healing from the Lord we must first make sure that we are in a right relationship with God. This means of healing grace belongs particularly to the Church of Jesus Christ. It is bequeathed to the believer, the true child of God.

I want you to notice something else too, of great importance. The sick are instructed to call for the elders of the church, not the elders to call for the sick. The instruction is clearly defined: *'Is any sick among you? let him* [i.e. the sick one] *call for the elders of the church; and let them* [the elders] *pray over him, anointing him with oil in the name of the Lord'*. The Lord places the responsibility upon the sick believer to call for the elders of the church. I have frequently noticed within the church that it is the pastor, or the minister, who usually calls the sick to come forward for prayer and anointing. Let me stress again that Scripture makes it unmistakably clear that the sick themselves are instructed to request the anointing with oil and prayer. Anointing with oil symbolises the healing power of the Holy Spirit. One is anointed with oil in the name of the Lord Jesus. The Christian believer will respect and revere this anointing, acknowledging that healing comes through the ministry and the person of the Holy Spirit. That is why it is essential, before we are anointed with oil, that our hearts must be clean and pure before the Lord.

My first personal experience of divine healing centred around the instruction in James 5:14. I was converted after a dramatic experience. I had lost my faith through a personal dilemma, but the Lord in His grace and mercy revealed Himself to me and I was reborn of the Spirit. I was brought to Christ during a severe illness, and even after my conversion I still needed the healing grace of Jesus. One evening in my desperation I turned to the Bible for encouragement. You can imagine my great joy when I opened the Bible at random at the chapter 5 of the letter of James.

As I began reading my eyes lighted on verse 14: *'Is any sick among you? let him call for the elders of the church'*.

I decided there and then to act upon this instruction. I requested the elders from a little Methodist church to visit me. My knowledge of church government was strictly limited in those days, and so I was rather disappointed when two dedicated elders came from the local chapel and I discovered one of there was quite young in age. I always imagined elders were the aged members of the church. I then directed the elders to the scriptures and requested them to anoint me with oil and pray the prayer of faith. It was at this point that I realised that I had overlooked the oil, so I asked the younger elder to go downstairs and fetch the little can of oil from the cycle shed. You can imagine my joy and surprise when he re-appeared with the oil and I discovered that the name of the brand was 'Three-in-one'!

The elders asked me how much oil to apply? I replied, 'Give me a liberal anointing!' So they poured the oil upon my head, and as it started running down my face so God's blessing fell upon me. I felt the mighty Spirit of God surging through me, and then the Lord's presence intensified until every atom of my being seemed to tingle with new life, energy and power. As I opened my eyes and lifted them heavenward I was conscious of a divine presence enveloping my whole being. For some thirty minutes I was charged and re-charged with the power of God. The Lord quickened me from the crown of my head to the soles of my feet, and within half an hour I rose up from my sickbed and dressed. I was still feeling a little weak having been bed-ridden for some days, but I knew within my spirit that the Lord had begun a tremendous work of healing in my body. Within a few weeks my normal strength returned. Every evidence of sickness disappeared and I was able to return to business once again, filled with praise and glory to God for my wonderful healing.

The ministry of the anointing with oil and the prayer of faith has always been very precious to me. Often I am requested to visit the sick and it is always a privilege to anoint with oil and offer the prayer of faith in the name of Jesus.

The third ministry of divine healing is to be found in Acts 19:11–12, where Paul prayed for handkerchiefs before they were laid on the sick.

It would be helpful to briefly look at the background of this unusual event. The apostle Paul was visiting Ephesus where he discovered a number of disciples who had been baptised unto John's baptism. Paul asked them if they believed in the Lord Jesus Christ, having preached the gospel to them. Afterwards he baptised them in water, laid his hands upon them and they were filled with the Holy Spirit. Paul continued disputing and persuading them concerning the things of the kingdom of God. During his stay in Asia, we read in Acts 19:11–12:

'God wrought special miracles by the hands of Paul: So that from his body were brought unto the sick handkerchiefs or aprons, and the diseases departed from them, and the evil spirits went out of them.'

Maybe the apostle blessed and anointed the handkerchiefs and aprons with oil in the name of the Lord, before returning them to the sick and suffering. These items were simply used as a point of contact to replace the personal laying on of hands by the Apostle Paul. As they were laid upon the sick in the name of the Lord Jesus, God honoured the faith of Paul and of the individual who needed healing and blessing accordingly.

It is over thirty years since the Holy Spirit first directed me to restore this specialised ministry of divine healing. I have lost count of the requests I have received. Along with each anointed handkerchief I send clear scriptural instructions. The sufferer is made to understand the need for a right relationship with the Lord Jesus, for if we regard iniquity in our heart the Lord will not hear us. I believe this special Bible ministry is available today. No doubt it meets the special needs of the many sick and suffering who are unable to make personal contact with me. I can imagine the apostle Paul receiving the handkerchiefs and aprons, lifting them up in his hands to the Lord, praying over them with authority and then giving clear instructions before returning them to the sick and the suffering.

I was ministering once in a small town in South Wales. I make frequent visits to this locality and there is always a good number attending the service. During my previous service a man suffering with a stroke had been miraculously healed and the news of his recovery spread through the community. When I arrived on this occasion there was a capacity congregation.

Just before the service began a Christian friend said to me, 'I have a close neighbour and friend who is seriously ill with cancer, and it is just a question of time before she goes into hospital for major surgery. I wonder if it will be possible for you to come round and visit her after the service?'

As the service continued late into the evening I proposed to the Christian friend that I would anoint a handkerchief with oil and send it to the sick neighbour in the name of the Lord Jesus. He promptly produced a pocket handkerchief which I anointed with oil in the name of the Lord. The congregation assisted with prayer and we all believed together that the sick one would receive healing from the Lord. Two weeks later, I was ministering in the same locality when the same Christian friend handed me a letter. I discovered it was a letter of testimony concerning his neighbour who was suffering with cancer. Within the space of an hour of receiving the anointed handkerchief there was an amazing improvement in her condition. Seventy-two hours later she attended the hospital to be informed that there was no trace of her cancerous lump. The letter gave full details of how the power of God had miraculously healed every trace of cancer.

And so our wonderful Lord continues to use the prayer handkerchief ministry in this day and age to bless and heal the sick and the suffering for His glory.

Chapter 11

Praying for the Sick

Intercessory prayer is also a positive divine healing ministry. Most days I receive numerous requests by letter and telephone from those earnestly desiring prayer for their recovery. These requests are carefully recorded so that during my personal times of intercession I can bring these urgent needs before the throne of grace. Our faithful prayer secretary notifies various prayer groups throughout the nation to join with me in this most vital intercessory ministry for the sick and suffering.

Jesus said:

'If two of you shall agree on earth as touching any thing that they shall ask, it shall be done for them of my Father which is in heaven.'   (Matthew 19:19)

Believers praying and agreeing together greatly assist the healing of the sick. Intercessory prayer is greatly effective. When prayer is offered the disease should be rebuked in the all-authoritative name of Jesus. That is a positive prayer based upon Christ's total victory at Calvary. The prayer of faith is the prayer that resists the infirmity, rebukes the sickness and expels the spirit of affliction. The prayer of faith is based upon the Word of God and channels its authority through these promises. Intercessory prayer is not so much pleading with God to heal the sick, but rather taking authority over the afflictions and rebuking them in the name of the Lord. Jesus accomplished total victory at Calvary over all sin and sickness. Intercessory prayer exploits this victory to the fullest extent. It is based upon a victory already consummated at the cross. It is always a positive prayer exercising authority over all sickness and disease. I pray for the sick and the suffering, with Christ's delegated authority commanding the sickness and disease to depart in the name of the Lord Jesus. The prayer of faith destroys the disease and expels the infirmity.

Jesus said, *'whatsoever ye shall ask of the Father in my name, he may give it you'* (John 15:16). The phrase 'in My name' suggests 'as My ambassador'. An ambassador is one sent with authority. So the prayer of faith is the prayer of authority, exercising total and complete power over every sickness and disease.

We will now consider the Holy Communion service as a way of receiving divine healing. Let us refer to Exodus chapter 12. This event introduces the 'passover lamb' from which the passover service was inaugurated. The children of Israel had been in bondage in Egypt for over four hundred years. The successive Pharaohs put great pressure upon them and they became a nation of slaves. The children of Israel cried to God for deliverance and the Lord remembered the covenant that He had made with Abraham, Isaac and Jacob. Moses was sent from the land of Midian to lead the children of Israel out of bondage, but it was necessary for the Lord God to judge the land of Egypt with many severe judgements. The tenth great judgement resulted in the death of the firstborn of man and beast. To preserve the children of Israel from this horrific judgement the Lord gave them special instructions. First, they were to take a lamb from among the flock. The lamb was to be without blemish, a male of the first year. This passover lamb was a type of the Lord Jesus Christ, the Lamb of God who was to bear away the sin of the world. The lamb was chosen on the tenth day and sacrificed on the fourteenth day. The life blood was caught in a basin and sprinkled with hyssop upon the lintel and the doorpost of their homes. This was a sign to the death angels, and when they were confronted by the blood sprinkled upon the doors they passed over without harming the occupants within. That is why this service is called the passover service. Judgement 'passed over' because the blood of the lamb was sprinkled upon their homes. We can also be saved from judgement if we confess our sin and ask for the cleansing blood of Jesus to purify our hearts. As with the blood of the passover lamb the blood of Jesus must be applied by faith to the heart to ensure the forgiveness of sins and the experience of personal salvation.

Notice, however, that the Israelites took another step of obedience. The body of the lamb was roasted with fire and eaten by members of the household. According to the psalmist, when they ate the body of the lamb there was not one weak or feeble person among their tribes. In other words, the eating of the body of the lamb provided divine health and strength. In fact, during this incident the Lord God provided both the spiritual and physical needs of His people.

Our present Holy Communion service has its origin in the passover service. Our Lord Jesus introduced the first service of communion during the Passover Feast in Jerusalem, the evening before He was crucified. The disciples of Jesus had gathered for the passover and our Lord joined them. The passover table would contain a number of items that reminded them of the events in Egypt in Exodus chapter 12. Jesus took up two of these items, namely the unleavened bread and one of the cups of wine and introduced the communion service with these words:

> *'And as they were eating, Jesus took bread, and blessed it, and brake it, and gave it to the disciples, and said, Take, eat, this is my body. And he took the cup, and gave thanks, and gave it to them, saying, Drink ye all of it; For this is my blood of the new testament, which is shed for many for the remission of sins. But I say unto you, I will not drink henceforth of this fruit of the vine, until that day when I drink it new with you in my Father's kingdom.'* (Matthew 26:26–29)

Notice carefully the two passover emblems Jesus took on this occasion to represent the new covenant blessings. First, He took the unleavened bread. The unleavened bread was a type of the body of the pascal lamb. The pascal lamb was without spot and blemish; pure, clean, with no sign of deformity. The unleavened bread betokens wholeness and purity. The body of the pascal lamb was a type of the body of our Lord Jesus Christ. Jesus said *'this is my body, which is given for you'* (Luke 22:19). His body was broken and His flesh torn by the nailprints, the crown of thorns and the spear which was thrust into His side. As we examine the body of our Lord Jesus we see clearly the bleeding wounds of the covenant. Isaiah referring to these scourge marks, declares *'with his stripes we are healed'* and again in 1 Peter 2:24 the apostle states *'by whose stripes ye were healed'*. So our Lord's scourged body covenants health and healing to all who believe, and when we attend the Holy Communion service the unleavened bread betokens God's grace of divine healing. As we take the bread we can use this as our point of contact, enabling us to receive healing and strength from the risen Lord Jesus. Wonderful testimonies have been reported by Christians having received divine healing at the Lord's table. If only every pastor and priest would emphasize this glorious truth at the Holy Communion service.

The apostle Paul goes on to say:

> *'...not discerning the Lord's body. For this cause many are weak and sickly among you...'*
>
> (1 Corinthians 11:29–30)

If we fail to appropriate the healing and strength provided by our Lord's body, then many will remain sick and weakly. But if we rightly discern our Lord's body and see our diseases and sicknesses laid upon Jesus, then every communicant has the right to the redemptive blessing of divine healing. How graciously the Lord provides so many varied ministries of divine healing. Whatever the sickness and affliction there is a scriptural provision for healing and deliverance.

Chapter 12

Why Some Are Not Healed

There are a variety of reasons why some are not healed. Maybe the major reason is an unwillingness on the part of the sufferer to make an outright commitment to the Lord Jesus. I have known a few cases where an unrepentant sinner has received some temporary benefit but the blessing has soon evaporated. Jesus graciously warned those who were healed *'sin no more, lest a worse thing come upto thee'* (John 5:14).

The Bible also states, if we regard iniquity in our hearts, the Lord will not hear us (Psalm 66:18). We cannot expect God to heal us if we continue in wilful sin.

Sometimes a particular sin may promote the sickness. The smoking habit, for example, may result in lung cancer. Continual stress and worry may spark off a mental breakdown. Relentless over-strain may bring on a stroke or a seizure. So the Lord may withhold healing because of some particular sin or unclean habit.

An elderly evangelical Christian suffered for many years with a recurring stomach ulcer. He frequently requested prayer from those endowed with the gift of healing, but he failed to recover. During this period he was often convicted about his deep spiritual need of water baptism. This he declined for a number of reasons. One day, however, the Spirit of God strongly challenged him on the issue and he finally condescended to be baptised. After submitting to the Lord's ordinance of water baptism he noticed a distinct improvement in his health. Three months later it became apparent that his stomach ulcer had disappeared and subsequent x-rays proved this. He then began testifying to the healing grace of God, for having submitted in obedience to the will of God he was miraculously healed.

A business associate, having failed to receive divine healing, sought my counsel. After prayerfully considering his position he confessed to a wilful sin in his life. Sincerely repenting he promised early restitution. I was able to minister to him with great confidence in the name of the Lord Jesus. Within moments he was healed of his rheumatic condition and he returned home glorifying God. Unconfessed sin or an unforgiving spirit (Matthew 6:15), iniquity in the heart (Proverbs 28:13; Psalm 66:18) are some of the reasons why some fail to receive divine healing. In such instances one must sincerely seek the Lord's forgiveness and make restitution where necessary. We are assured:

> *'If we confess our sins, he is faithful and just to forgive us our sins, and to cleanse us from all unrighteousness.'* (1 John 1:9)

Another reason why some fail to receive healing is because they have little regard for natural laws. If we abuse our bodies, our natural resources, we are inviting trouble. To 'burn the candle at both ends' may result in nervous exhaustion or a complete mental and physical breakdown. God may grant supernatural strength in special circumstances but if we persistently fail to observe the natural health codes serious consequences may result. We must learn self-control, watch our eating habits and live sensibly for the glory of God.

Others fail to receive divine healing because they cast away their confidence when the symptoms persist. They present themselves in good faith for prayer, then appeal to their feelings and senses for evidence of healing, instead of firmly fixing their confidence in the promise of God. Our feelings are so changeable: one moment we may feel elated and the next disillusioned and discouraged. Our feelings at their best are not reliable. One thing is certain: the promises of God are steadfast and sure. Immediately following the healing prayer we should act upon Mark 11:24 – Jesus said:

> *'Therefore I say unto you, What things soever ye desire, when ye pray, believe that ye receive them, and ye shall have them.'*

Instead of appealing to our feelings we must hold steadfast to the word of God. Our unwavering confession should always be: **God says it, I believe it, that settles it.**

Some fail to receive divine healing because they confuse hope with faith. When asked 'do you believe the Lord can heal you?' They reply, 'I hope so.' The fundamental difference between hope and faith is a question of tense. Faith is always identified with the present while hope is always looking to the future. Hope looks forward to future realisation while faith activates in the present.

When Jesus returned to Bethany after the death of Lazarus, Martha went out to meet Him. She said unto Jesus, *'Lord, if thou hadst been here, my brother had not died'* (John 11:21). Martha was convinced that if Jesus had arrived while Lazarus was still alive the Master would have healed him. In other words, Martha had faith for yesterday. When Jesus went on to reassure her, *'thy brother shall rise again'* (John 11:23), Martha's faith now turns to hope. She said unto Jesus, *'I know that he shall rise again in the resurrection at the last day'* (John 11:24).

In other words, Martha found it impossible to believe that Jesus would raise Lazarus in the present, but she hoped he would be raised at the last day. Martha only hoped – she did not believe.

Abraham also experienced the same conflict between faith and hope. We read in the Scriptures that Abraham **believed against hope**. Abraham looked forward in hope to the fulfilment of God's promises and that he would receive a son and heir. When Abraham's hope turned to faith God miraculously fulfilled His promise. So hoping must give way to believing.

In Mark 11:24 Jesus said,

> *'Therefore I say unto you, What things soever ye desire, when ye pray, believe that ye receive them, and ye shall have them.'*

This is one of the most vital faith verses in the New Testament. Read it again and again in order to appreciate its meaning. Notice the point of appropriation – *'when ye pray'*. In other words the very moment we pray we are to adopt an attitude of uncompromising faith, believing that we are already receiving what we have asked for. *'When ye pray'*, of course is the precise moment we pray. This point in time is always present tense, in the 'Now'. So our hearts are to take hold of the answer to our prayer the moment we pray. Granted we may not experience an immediate answer but nevertheless we are to believe in our hearts that we are receiving what we have asked for. This act of believing gears our confidence to present tense realities. It is no longer, 'I hope so' but 'Amen, it is so'. That is the voice of receiving faith.

Now some fail to receive divine healing because their confidence in God wavers.

> *'But let him ask in faith, nothing wavering. For he that wavereth is like a wave of the sea driven with the wind and tossed. For let not that man think he shall receive any thing from the Lord. A double minded man is unstable in all his ways.'*
>
> (James 1:6–8)

It is so easy to open a faith account with God full of zeal and enthusiasm. It is quite another matter, however, to hold fast to the confession of our faith until we receive the full healing we are believing for. Naaman, the Syrian general, faced this problem when he was commanded by the prophet Elisha to wash seven times in the River Jordan. Joshua and the children of Israel found themselves under orders to march around the formidable walls of Jericho seven consecutive days proving they did not receive an immediate answer to their faith. Faith may run high in a spiritual atmosphere charged with divine expectancy, but true believing is certainly tested in the climate of opposition and a prolonged wait.

A Christian sister suffering with osteo-arthritis was effectively blessed in one of our central London services. She laid aside her walking stick and ran around the church glorifying God. At the termination of the service she shook my hand saying 'God has really blessed me tonight, but please continue to pray for me.' When I asked for what purpose, she replied, 'every time I get a healing touch from God the devil comes around and robs me of my blessing.' Her faith in the Lord began wavering in spite of the amazing blessing God had granted her. She anticipated losing her healing almost as soon as she had received it. Her faith was like the wave of the sea driven with the wind and tossed. She should have consolidated her faith by holding fast to her confession of God's promise. Her confidence should have remained steadfast and unmoveable, abounding in the knowledge of God's unfailing faithfulness. The initial blessing of the Lord is often a token of God's goodness, which can blossom into full fruition if we hold fast to the confession of our faith without wavering. The 'holding fast' process involves a determined effort to stand firm on the promises of God. It also identifies with a positive confession, uncompromising action, and a giving of thanks until all symptoms have disappeared. Further prayer can be requested to accelerate the healing process, but this must always be accompanied with the continuing confession that God is already at work healing and blessing. This confession must always be based upon the promises of God and not on our feelings. Jesus promised:

'Heaven and earth shall pass away: but my words shall not pass away.' (Luke 21:33)

Chapter 13

Paul's Thorn in the Flesh

One of the most prevalent objections raised today against the ministry of Divine Healing is 'Paul's Thorn in the Flesh'. One traditional idea has led to another. The widespread teaching that God is the author of special diseases, and that He desires some of the most devout of His children to remain sick and diseased as a means of them exhibiting fortitude and patience, has no doubt been derived from the supposition that Paul had a disease which God refused to heal. Thousands of precious people are suffering needlessly today believing it is pleasing to God for them to suffer so.

In order to have a true scriptural understanding of this matter let us consider exactly what the Bible says about this 'thorn in the flesh'. First the expression **'thorn in the flesh'** is only used throughout the Scriptures as an **expression** or **illustration**. Not once is it used as a figure of **sickness**: e.g. Numbers 33:55 . . . the expression 'thorns in your sides' here refers to the inhabitants of Canaan; Joshua 23:13 – here again the expression refers to the heathen nations of Canaan. Both of these times the Bible states clearly what the thorns were. Just as clearly, Paul states exactly what his thorn was – *'the messenger of Satan'* (2 Corinthians 12:7).

The Messenger of Satan

'The messenger of Satan' is translated by others as the 'angel of the Devil'. Again this illustration is a personality. The word 'messenger' is translated from the Greek word *'angelos'* which appears 188 times in the Bible, and is translated 181 times as an 'angel'. In every case it is a **personality** and not a **thing**. Preachers have labelled Paul's 'thorn in the flesh' as everything from an oriental eye disease to an unconverted wife. However, Paul says his thorn was a 'messenger or an angel of Satan'. (See Matthew 25:41.)

To Buffet Me

Next, Paul says exactly what the 'thorn in the flesh' came to **do**. He says the 'angel of Satan' came to buffet me. The word 'buffet' means 'blow upon blow', e.g. waves buffeting a ship. (See also Matthew 26:67.) It suggests … Beaten with many blows and would perfectly suggest the harassing work of an 'angel of the devil'. We find that Paul definitely suffered cruelly at the hands of the world:

- attempted murder (Acts 9:23)
- mobbed (Acts 13:50)
- stoned and left for dead (Acts 14:19)
- beaten and jailed (Acts 16:22)
- tried in court five times (e.g. Acts 16:20)
- shipwrecked (Acts 27:27–44)

(See also 2 Corinthians chapters 6 and 11 where we have further details and many more examples.)

Who but an angel of Satan could be responsible for this?

Certainly, Paul's thorn could not be defective eyesight, for we read **God healed him** of blindness in Acts 9:18.

Finally, God replied to Paul's persistent prayer for deliverance: *'My grace is sufficient for thee'* (2 Corinthians 12:9). Grace surely is a ministration to the soul. God did not say My **health** is sufficient for thee. Some refer to Galatians 6:11 as a means of supposing Paul had defective eyesight: *'Ye see how large a letter I have written unto you with mine own hand.'* The word 'letter' here is translated from the same Greek word as used in 2 Corinthians 3:6 and does not mean a letter in the alphabet. Secondly, the word 'large' used here means the quantitative form and is not the kind of large used to express **size** but **quantity**. Paul undoubtedly speaks of his epistle as a long one. It was not the usual custom to write his own.

Again in Galatians 4:15, we read,

> *'I bear you record, that, if it had been possible, ye would have plucked out your eyes, and have given them me.'*

This scripture is supposed to prove that Paul's eyes were diseased and that people were willing to give him their own eyes to replace his diseased ones. This is only **supposition** and has **no scriptural foundation**. There is no doubt that this expression was in common use and was made by the Galatians as an expression of affection and love to Paul. There are many such expressions today, e.g. 'I would cut off my right hand and give it to you.' Certainly this would not prove I had cancer in my hand.

Having examined the main scriptures concerning this matter may we finally turn to Matthew 8:17 to see **that just as Jesus bore our sins so he bears our sicknesses**. What God put on Jesus He does not put on you and me. Claim your heritage of full health now!

Chapter 14

Taking God at His Word

I was ministering in South Yorkshire in one of the local Baptist churches. A young lad of 8 years came forward for the laying on of hands. His mother rolled up the boy's sleeve which revealed the irritating scourge of weeping excema.

'Is Jesus going to heal you?' I asked.

The young lad replied with confidence, 'Of course He is.'

Four weeks later I returned to the same venue. The boy pushed his way through the crowded aisle and came to me.

'It's all gone!' he testified smiling with satisfaction.

'Let me look at your arms.' I asked.

The young fellow slipped off his jacket and rolled up his sleeves. His arm was perfectly healed. All that remained were the stains on the skin where the excema had been.

'And who made you better?' I enquired.

'Jesus did it!' he replied.

As the young boy rejoined his mother I lifted my heart heavenward and thanked God for the faith of a little child.

About the same period I was invited to conduct a special divine healing service on the outskirts of

Birmingham. The venue was the local library. It was filled to capacity. First I preached a simple gospel message inviting those present to turn from sin to Christ. Many responded and gave public declaration of their desire to receive Jesus as their Saviour. Suddenly a young mongol child appeared, attired in a beautiful white dress.

As I walked near to her she was suddenly overwhelmed by the power of God. She sank to the floor under the anointing of the Holy Spirit. Her mother witnessing the scene came forward to assist her daughter. I assured her that all was in order and that the Lord's anointing was upon her child. A few minutes later there was great excitement. The mother of the mongol child raised her hands and shouted.

'It's a miracle! It's a miracle!'

The local pastor went to investigate. We quickly discovered that the youngster had been miraculously healed of a large swelling. It had suddenly disappeared. As we examined her arm there was no trace of the offending affliction. When the assembled company became aware of this amazing event they rejoiced and clapped their hands, glorifying God.

As mother and daughter returned to their seats I again lifted my heart to heaven and thanked God for the faith of a little child. Oh, if only our faith were more simple and childlike.

During one of our memorable open-air crusades in West Africa a charabang of youngsters was conveyed to the service. I was informed that many of them were deaf and dumb. The Holy Spirit guided me to invite the local ministers and elders to assist with the blessing of the children. As they lined up in front of the platform I called the vast congregation to prayer.

In the all-prevailing name of Jesus the deaf and dumb afflictions were authoritatively cast out. The wonderful power of God fell upon us.

Soon the atmosphere was electrified with excitement. One by one the deaf and dumb children were miraculously healed. A young boy was lifted to the platform – Jesus had opened his deaf ears. His young eyes were filled with wonder and amazement. He began speaking.

'Dada, Mummy, Jesus.'

Another shout of praise from the congregation. I was later informed that twenty-two deaf and dumb children during that memorable service had received hearing and spoken clearly for the first time.

Those amazing scenes will always remain with me. Once again I sighed, 'Oh, for the faith of a child.'

Have you witnessed the simple uncomplicated confidence of these little ones? They just take you at face value.

They remind me of a simple but profound saying which provided me with faith over many years:

'God says it! I believe it! That settles it!'

It is worth repeating:

'God says it! I believe it! That settles it!'

In today's complicated world we love to probe, question and analyse. Our natural reasoning and often our complicated knowledge of spiritual issues can easily becloud our faith. We rapidly lose touch with that simplified faith which moves the heart of God.

The first miracle that Jesus performed was based on a simple act of obedience. Mary, the mother of Jesus, gave this childlike instruction to the servants at the wedding feast:

'Whatsoever he saith unto you, do it.'   (John 2:5)

Implicit obedience resulted in Jesus turning the water into wine. Later Jesus instructed a blind man to go to the pool of Siloam and wash.

'He went his way therefore, and washed, and came seeing.'   (John 9:7)

The blind man later testified:

'A man that is called Jesus made clay, and anointed mine eyes, and said unto me, Go to the pool of Siloam, and wash: and I went and washed, and I received sight.'   (John 9:11)

Oh the wonder of it all! The simplicity of faith in God. The Master Healer commanded a palsied man to rise, take up his bed and walk. As the afflicted man obeyed the word of Jesus he was miraculously healed.

It all seems so simple. But faith in God is simple. It is with childlike simplicity we believe. The laying on of hands is the simplest of acts.

When I lay my hands upon the sick and suffering in the wonderful name of the Lord I often contemplate – how uncomplicated are the instructions of Jesus. Oh, if our faith were more simple, we would take God at His Word.

As I gently lay my hands upon the sick in the name of Jesus I am aware of the powerful anointing of the Holy spirit flowing through me. The laying on of hands is a simple faith contact which helps to release the mighty healing grace of God.

In other words I perform my simple task in obedience to the Lord, and then God takes over and performs mighty deeds.

To get to the heart of the matter, Divine Healing results from simple uncomplicated faith and an intimate relationship with the Lord. Many Christians allow their faith to become confused and entangled with doubts, questionings and reasonings.

Some will do almost everything and anything but exercise a simple, persistent, unwavering trust in God. When you present the scriptural revelation of Divine Healing they sometimes respond,

'But I know all that!'

How right they are! They do know in their minds and intellects the basic doctrine of divine healing but they have lost their simple faith in God.

At no time will the Christian reach a point where simple faith can be discarded and replaced by some other virtue. A detailed knowledge of Scriptures, evidence of spiritual maturity, and event the fruits of righteousness are no substitute for a simple unwavering faith.

'Without faith it is impossible to please him [God].*'*
(Hebrews 11:6)

Faith is an indispensable ingredient in our relationship with the Lord.

I have known godly folk endowed with the fruits of righteousness succumb to sickness and disease. When the real test came they lacked the simple unwavering faith that is so vital to healing.

How easy it is to turn to other sources for help when our faith in God is really tested. The Lord God entrusted Job with his serious situation. He knew that Job would stand fast in the face of the onslaught.

While all around suggested that Job *'Curse God and die'* the Lord's servant faithfully declared, *'I will praise God and live.'* Job held fast to his faith without wavering. He never doubted the outcome.

'In all this did not Job sin with his lips.' (Job 2:10)

He believed with childlike faith:

'Thou shalt come to thy grave in a full age, like as a shock of corn cometh in in his season.'
(Job 5:26)

In the height of his conflict Job cried:

'Though he slay me, yet will I trust in him.'
(Job 13:15)

This is the confession of one who loves the Lord absolutely and trusts him perfectly.

Can God trust you with your situation? Maybe you are troubled, anxious, fearful, sick and afflicted?

What a wonderful opportunity to put your complete trust in God. What a golden opportunity to prove the faithfulness of the Lord. Let your faith thrive on your problems by taking them to the Lord in prayer. Feed your faith on God's promises. Strengthen your faith by looking to God's Word for healing and deliverance. Draw closer to the Lord and trust Him absolutely.

'And the Lord, *he it is that doth go before thee; he will be with thee, he will not fail thee, neither forsake thee: fear not, neither be dismayed.'*
(Deuteronomy 31:8)

'There hath not failed one word of all his good promise.'
(1 Kings 8:56)

Ask the Holy Spirit to guide you into the Word of God. Look to the Scriptures for revelation and guidance. Do not strain or strive – allow the Lord time to guide you through His Word. Wait before Him. Take time to listen to the voice of the Master. He has the divine solution to all your problems. Read your Bible under the inspiration of the Holy Spirit. The Lord will impress His truth upon your redeemed spirit.

Jesus said:

> *'If ye continue in my word, then are ye my disciples indeed: and ye shall know the truth, and the truth shall make you free.'* (John 8:31–32)

Chapter 15

Healing
Through God's Word

I received a telephone call from a Christian friend. Her dear husband had recently died. Now her dog companion, Tiny, had become very sick. She telephoned in desperation.

'The vet says nothing can be done. Please, please help me.'

As I prayerfully pondered her request I lifted my heart to heaven for divine guidance and instruction. The Holy Spirit came to my rescue, reminding me of the **word of the Lord:**

*'For the earnest expectation of **the creature** waiteth for the manifestation of the sons of God.'*

(Romans 8:19)

This scriptural direction prompted me to bless a prayer cloth according to Acts 19:11–12. Using this as a point of contact the suffering animal was miraculously restored. At our next Central London Service the grateful friend presented her dog, fit and well, testifying of God's goodness and faithfulness. The outstanding issue in this case was undoubtedly **implicit** obedience to the word of the Lord.

Blessing, healing and miracles are the divine response to our **uncompromising** obedience to the word and will of God.

It is vital that we seek the mind of the Lord and then obey His word without faltering.

I was asked to visit a young wife seriously ill in a West Wales hospital. I was informed that she was seriously paralysed and receiving treatment in an intensive care unit. My time with her was strictly limited. I consulted the Lord for His mind on the issue. The Holy Spirit promptly brought to my heart a verse from the Scriptures:

> *'The* Lord *is the strength of my* [thy] *life.'*
>
> (Psalm 27:1)

I conveyed this special message to the young woman. Afterwards she testified that this heaven-inspired word had taken root in her subconscious mind and was the turning point of her miraculous recovery.

I was seventeen years of age when I took ill. For many weeks I was confined to bed with nervous exhaustion and a breakdown. My spirits were very low and my mind confused. One evening I was desperately depressed and decided to sink down on my knees. I earnestly prayed to God about my predicament. The Lord was gracious to me. He granted me a remarkable vision of the cross and my crucified Saviour. The gracious words of Jesus, *'Father forgive them'* pierced my soul. Jesus immediately imparted a deep peace to my heart. His presence flooded my being. A steadfast assurance settled in my heart and I knew Jesus had saved me. Tears of joy and release were followed with a profound sense of gratitude. From that hour Jesus became real to me. I was able to hold intimate fellowship with the Lord. His abiding presence became a reality. I could confide in Him and share the deepest yearnings of my heart. This new and living relationship with Jesus gave birth to a miracle of Divine Healing. A few days after my conversion I was asking the Lord to reveal His healing truth to me and was distinctly prompted by the Holy Spirit to take up my Bible and open its pages before the Lord. As I did so my eyes lightened on the following verses:

> *'Is any among you afflicted? let him pray. Is any merry? let him sing psalms. Is any sick among you? let him call for the elders of the church; and let them pray over him, anointing him with oil in the name of the Lord: And the prayer of faith shall save the sick, and the Lord shall raise him up; and if he have committed sins, they shall be forgiven him. Confess your faults one to another, and pray one for another, that ye may be healed. The effectual fervent prayer of a righteous man availeth much.'*
>
> (James 5:13–16)

I could hardly believe my eyes as I read the scriptures a second and a third time. The Lord was giving me clear and definite instructions how to be healed by His power.

The elders arrived from the local church and I pointed out to them that they had been called in response to James 5:14. They were willing to obey the scriptures and anoint me with oil. They liberally anointed me and began to pray positively. Within seconds the power of God flowed through my being like electricity. I was charged with new life. Waves of blessing quickened every fibre of my being. The release was so thrilling that I was filled with joy. I promptly rose up from my sick-bed and carefully made my way downstairs. My appetite returned and subsequently my strength. Within days I returned to my place of employment well and strong.

I was raised up by the power of God and healed by my risen Lord. When I contemplate this miracle I am aware that it resulted from simply **taking God at His word.**

For over fifty years I have been engaged actively in the service of the Lord. During this demanding period I have enjoyed remarkable. health and I would like to set forth the following reasons:

1. **A long-term commitment to Christ**
   Just after my conversion I entered into a sacred covenant with the Lord. I surrendered my life to His will and purpose. I ceased to have any claim upon myself and yielded my all to Jesus. By His grace I have maintained this long-term commitment to Christ.

2. **A positive reaction to illness**
   Whenever the symptoms of some complaint have appeared I have promptly and authoritatively resisted them in the name of Jesus. With the same spiritual determination I resist temptation so I resist sickness. I refuse to allow my body to be the habitation of any sickness or disease. Sometimes the symptoms may linger but I firmly rebuke and resist them until they completely disappear.

3. **When the symptoms persist**
   Only once have the symptoms of an affliction persisted. I sought the Lord with all my heart and He informed me that I was overtaxing my body. When I obeyed His voice and rested

awhile the Lord graciously renewed my strength and I was healed.

4. **Filled with power and authority**
To enable me to make an authoritative stand against sickness the Lord filled me with the Holy Spirit and great power. I strongly recommend that all Christians seek to be baptized in the Holy Spirit and utilize the authority available through the name and precious blood of Jesus.

5. **It is essential to eat correctly**
The Lord taught me numerous lessons about my eating habits. Wholesome food is essential to sound health as well as rest and sleep. It is also beneficial to fast and pray as the Lord directs.

6. **Exercise and fresh air**
I endeavour to walk at least ten miles weekly. A brisk walk into the country will stimulate the circulation, freshen the cheeks and loosen the limbs.

7. **Claim divine health daily**
Every day I claim Divine Health from the Lord. I claim His protection against all sickness and disease. He has promised:

'There shall no evil befall thee, neither shall any plague come nigh thy dwelling.'   (Psalm 91:10)

'The righteous shall flourish like a palm tree ... They shall bring forth fruit in old age.'
(Psalm 92:12, 14)

Divine health is available as well as Divine Healing. The same wonderful Lord is the strength of my life and the health of my being.

If only we could take God at His Word and act with uncompromising faith upon His infallible promise.

One day a woman from the coast of Canaan came to Jesus on behalf of her daughter, who was grievously vexed by a demon. As she desperately sought this blessing she was confronted by total silence.

> *'But he answered her not a word.'*
>
> (Matthew 15:23)

How unlike Jesus! What had she done to deserve this treatment? Refusing to be discouraged, however, she turned to the Lord's disciples imploring their help. They also refused to assist, ordering her to go away. Determined to get help for her daughter, she returned a second time to Jesus. But Jesus answered:

> *'I am not sent but unto the lost sheep of the house of Israel.'*   (Matthew 15:24)

She returned yet again and fell down before Him and worshipped Him saying, *'Lord, help me.'* But Jesus replied:

> *'It is not meet to take the children's bread and cast it to dogs.'*   (Matthew 15:26)

A fourth time the woman laid claim to her daughter's deliverance.

> *'Then Jesus answered and said unto her, O woman, great is thy faith: be it unto thee even as thou wilt. And her daughter was made whole from that very hour.'*   (Matthew 15:28)

There is a faith which refuses to take **'no'** for an answer: a resolute, uncompromising determination to press through with God's promises; a refusing to let go until heaven has responded – until the answer comes. The early church prayed **without ceasing** until the Apostle Peter was delivered from prison.

This does not suggest a complicated drawn-out procedure but a simple unwavering determination to hold God to His Word. How easily we let go when the blessing is so near to hand. It must be emphasized that the most important aspect of divine healing is one's personal relationship with the Lord. Believing is receiving. While we maintain a believing attitude Jesus will direct His healing grace towards us. As the blessing of the Lord flows we are progressively quickened and restored.

When my natural resources are depleted, I simply relax in the presence of Jesus, allowing the waves of His power and glory to rejuvenate and revive me. It is like standing under a refreshing waterfall! I become saturated with His presence and power. The new wine of His Spirit restores my soul and quickens my mortal body. At first I simply imagine that I am touching the hem of my Saviour's garment. I reach my hand to heaven in childlike faith. I go through the motions of reaching out to touch the Lord. Then I simply accept the blessing of His healing grace and sure enough, His wonderful power becomes a reality. I refuse to leave the Lord's immediate presence until He saturates me with His divine virtue. While I maintain this blessed and intimate communion with Jesus, His resurrection life permeates my being.

There is nothing more wonderful this side of heaven than to experience the power of Jesus flowing through your being. Being occupied with the Lord is both health and healing. Again and again I reach out to heaven to receive the inflow of His power and grace. I refuse to let go until I am fully charged with His heaven-sent blessing.

While I maintain this blessed communion and contact with Jesus, the streams of living water refresh, revive and rejuvenate my soul, mind and body.

Chapter 16

Ascertaining the Will of God

Now we consider one of the most controversial aspects of Divine Healing – how to ascertain the will of God.

Many seeking Divine Healing question God's willingness to heal them, praying 'Lord, **if** it be thy will.'

First we must understand what is meant by the will of God. Jesus testified:

> 'Lo, I come **(in the volume of the book it is written of me,)** to do thy will, O God.'
>
> (Hebrews 10:7; see also Psalm 40:7)

Jesus committed Himself completely to the Father's will as it was revealed **through the Word of God.**

He received a perfect understanding of the **will of the Father** through the revelation of God's Word.

> 'Then answered Jesus and said unto them, Verily, verily, I say unto you, The Son can do nothing of himself, but what he seeth the Father do: for what things soever he doeth, these also doeth the Son likewise.'
>
> (John 5:19)

'The **works** I do – I see my Father do!'

So **God's will** is the revelation of His mind, plan and purpose. Jesus ascertained the will of God by reading and obeying the written word of God. Examine the text carefully:

> 'Lo, I come (**in the volume of the book** it is written of me,) to do thy will, O God.'
>
> (Hebrews 10:7; see also Psalm 40:7)

What did Jesus mean? Jesus referred to **'the book'** meaning the **Old Testament record**, i.e. the prophets, the psalms etc. The nouns 'testament' and 'will' in the English dictionary have one and the same meaning.

The 'Old Testament' and 'New Testament' really means the 'old will' and the 'new will' of God. **So the inspired Word of God is the will of God.**

Jesus received the revelation of God's will through reading the inspired word of God, i.e. the Old Testament writings. We are told *'All scripture is given by inspiration of God'* (2 Timothy 3:16). So if we desire to know the will of God we must read the 'testaments' for ourselves. With the assistance of the Holy Spirit we can easily discern the mind and the will of God as we prayerfully study the **Word of God.**

A leper once came to Jesus to be cured. Because of his limited knowledge of divine truth the leper said, *'Lord, **if thou wilt**, thou canst make me clean'* (Matthew 8:2). The leper did not doubt the power of Jesus to heal him but he did query God's **willingness** to cure him. How did Jesus respond?

> 'And Jesus put forth his hand, and touched him, saying, I will; be thou clean, And immediately his leprosy was cleansed.'   (Matthew 8:3)

It was essential for the leper first to understand that Jesus **willed to heal** him.

This incident reveals how vital it is to ascertain God's will **before** we pray for healing and deliverance. We can only approach the heavenly throne with confidence when we are certain of God's will in the matter. Jesus refers to the **will of God** in the special prayer He taught His disciples:

'Thy will be done in earth, as it is in heaven.'
(Matthew 6:10)

So the earthly pattern follows the heavenly. God's will in heaven is to be enacted here on earth. Seeing there is no sickness or disease in heaven we have a right to pray accordingly.

Finally, the healing of the leper reveals another truth. When offering the 'prayer of faith' there are two basic considerations. First, we must pray **into a knowledge of God's will** before we pray **God's will into reality**. There is no room within the context of the prayer of faith for the phrase 'if it be thy will'. This is a lazy prayer – usually offered by those who ignorantly or innocently fail to understand the basic principles of prayer. It is essential to possess a clear understanding of 'the will of God' **before** the prayer of faith is offered. There is little point in praying, **if we do not pray in conformity** with the perfect will of God. So before the prayer of faith we must first ascertain the will of God and then pray the will of God.

Many sincere Christians say 'I know God is **able** to heal but is He **willing** to heal me?'

The **personal revelation** of God's willingness to heal is an essential pre-requisite to divine healing. The prayer of faith is based upon a personal knowledge of the revealed will of God. I know an Anglican lady who has experienced divine healing on many occasions. She always asks these two questions:

- 'Lord why am I sick?'
- 'Lord, how do you intend to heal me?'

Then she consults the Lord Jesus and the Scriptures to find the answers. She will kneel before the Lord and open her Bible in His immediate presence. She prayerfully reads the Word of God until the Holy Spirit illuminates some particular portions of Scripture. Implicitly obeying His revealed word she is blessed and healed time and time again. If only we likewise would consult the word of the Lord more frequently. The Bible states – He sent **His word** and healed them.

> *'He sent his word and healed them, and delivered them from their destructions.'*   (Psalm 107:20)

Always remember God's Word is the revelation of His will. It is a lamp unto our feet and a light to our path. His word is Spirit and life. His Word is health and healing. That is why we should promptly consult the Word of God **the moment** we become the victims of sickness and disease.

What about those who believe they are suffering in the **will of God**? Many who take this attitude frequently reveal an inconsistent testimony. An arthritic sufferer tried to convince me that her infirmity was in the same category as Paul's thorn in the flesh. She fervently contended that she was suffering for the glory of God. When I proposed prayer for Divine Healing she declined saying,

'This is my cross and I must bear it. I am suffering for the glory of God.'

There was no doubting her sincerity. She really believed her affliction was heaven sent and that she had to endure it for the glory of God.

My next question, however, proved rather embarrassing. 'Are you seeking medical help for your complaint?'

'Oh yes' she replied. 'I have an excellent doctor and my tablets are doing me good.'

When I pointed out that her philosophy of suffering for the glory of God was completely contradicted by her attempts to be healed by other means, she saw the light.

Those who contend they are suffering for the glory of God should be content with their lot. The last thing they should do is seek healing by other means. In fact, this philosophy may even suggest that those suffering for the glory of God should desire even greater degrees of sickness in order to glorify God all the more.

This is completely illogical and totally contrary to the word and the will of God.

Chapter 17

How to Keep Your Healing

I received a letter from an arthritic sufferer who had attended one of my crusade services.

'Dear Brother Scothern,
I recently attended one of your services and received laying on of hands in the name of the Lord Jesus. The power of God fell upon me and I was overwhelmed and found myself lying on the floor. The spiritual experience was indescribable, and I went home rejoicing in the Lord, but to my disappointment I was not healed. Can you please explain this?'

I replied,

'Dear Christian Friend,
When we go forward to receive the laying on of hands it is with the desire of receiving healing from the living Lord. Now, healing is quite distinct from a miracle. Healing is a process of being cured. Healing is always progressive but a miracle usually occurs instantaneously. The verb "to heal" means "to get better, to recover", and this suggests progression. You may have expected a miracle but because nothing

happened immediately you cast away your confidence and allowed your disappointments to quench your faith. What you failed to recognise, however, was that the work of divine healing had begun. Yes, at that very moment that hands were laid upon you God began to fulfil His word and you began to recover. However, the moment you allowed your disappointment to undermine your confidence the divine healing process ceased. As you receive the laying on of hands in Jesus' name, the ministry of healing commences. If, however, you allow disappointment, doubt, or unbelief to undermine your faith, then immediately the divine healing process ceases. This process continues as long as we continue to hold a positive attitude of faith. So dear friend, because you allowed a negative attitude to stifle your faith, so the divine operation of the Holy Spirit ceased to heal your body. So I exhort you to make a fresh point of contact with the Lord Jesus, only next time, believe with all your heart that the healing work of grace is continuing in your body according to the word of the Lord.'

Another believer corresponded:

'Dear Brother Scothern,
I came to your service for divine healing and the Lord wonderfully healed me. Four weeks later I was still enjoying wonderful health but the other morning when I awoke, all the sickness had returned and I am very confused and disappointed I cannot understand why the sickness has returned, especially having been healed for so long. Please help me!'

Why do our sicknesses and diseases return? First, let me say that we have a very subtle and persistent enemy who will take every opportunity to make us sick or ill. He will tempt us to the limit by restoring the symptoms of some previous complaint. We may be tempted physically just like we are tempted spiritually. Temptation is Satan's initial approach. He goads or tempts us to sin. Temptation is not sin, but when we yield to temptation that is sin. If we resolutely resist the temptation we gain a mighty victory over sin and Satan. In the same way Satan may tempt us physically by placing certain symptoms upon us. When we have been healed by the Lord, Satan waits for a vulnerable moment and then places the symptoms upon us once again. We wake up one morning and discover the symptoms have returned. If we accept them without question we may quickly fall sick again. We must resist any returning symptoms as resolutely as we would resist spiritual temptation. The symptoms are often Satan's forerunner of disease. We must resist them, resolutely in the mighty name of Jesus.

I was wonderfully healed by the Lord Jesus during the first year of my conversion. One day without warning the old symptoms returned. Having been warned about this previously, I resisted the returning symptoms, commanding them to leave me in the name of Jesus. For some time the symptoms persisted but I resolutely refused to give in. I continued to give glory to God for my health, resisting the symptoms in the name of Jesus, by the blood of Jesus and with the weapon of praise. Within twenty-four hours the symptoms began to disappear and I found myself completely healed again. We must resist with all the weapons at our disposal. The Bible says that if we resist the enemy, he will flee from us. If our symptoms continue to persist in spite of all we do, then we must ask the Lord to guide us concerning what should be done next.

There were five porches at the healing pool of Bethsaida I will now suggest five ways to keep your healing. First, the Bible says we must walk by faith and not by sight. Sight, like feelings, is one of our natural senses. Often when I have prayed for someone they will say, 'Oh I don't feel any better,' or on the other hand they may say, 'I feel absolutely wonderful.' They base their testimony on human feelings, but human feelings are so contradictory. Something which may excite your feelings today may not create the same excitement tomorrow. Human feelings vary with the weather. In fact, they often vary by the moment. Therefore, our faith must not be based upon our feelings. Our faith and confidence must at all times be based upon the Word of God. Our feelings are so changeable but God's Word remains steadfast and sure. Jesus said, *'Heaven and earth shall pass away, but my words shall not pass away'* (Matthew 24:35). They only sure foundation for our faith is what God has decreed and declared.

I know a lady who attended one of my services and she was very ill with a cancerous growth. I prayed for her in the name of the Lord Jesus and commanded the cancerous growth to die. From that moment her confession was **'with the stripes of Jesus I am healed'**. When people asked her how she was healed or how she was getting better she would say, 'I am wholly leaning on the promises of God, and God has promised me that with His stripes I am healed'. In other words, she was not governed by her feelings. There were days when she felt better, and there were days when she felt worse. But at all times her confession, her attitude, was positive and unwavering. 'With His stripes I am healed,' she would say, again and again. In the end the Lord miraculously healed her. She walked by faith instead of her feelings. Our feelings are not generally a safe guide. We walk by faith by taking God at His word. We see our sicknesses and diseases legally laid upon Jesus. We claim our healing and health by faith, at all times believing that what God says is absolutely true. Do not base your faith on your feelings but upon the wonderful Word of God.

Now we consider the second truth. Having been prayed for we must hold fast to the confession of faith without wavering. We must believe at the moment of blessing that the Lord's healing grace and power has become effective in us. We must believe that the healing grace of Jesus has already taken effect.

Jesus said,

> '*When ye pray* [that is the moment you pray], *believe ye have received them* [what you asked for], *and ye shall receive them* [it].'   (Mark 11:24)

We must hold fast to this confession without wavering.

Our faith rises or falls according to the level of our confession. If we talk negatively, so our faith is undermined. If we confess positively, our faith is encouraged. Talking about our sicknesses and symptoms must be kept to a minimum; we must cease confessing that our sickness is having an advantage over us. We must cease looking within, at the signs, the symptoms and the weaknesses and begin looking to the Lord. We must continually give thanks for the process of divine healing, believing that it has already begun in our bodies. We accept this glorious truth that the Lord is already at work within us, healing and quickening our mortal bodies. Our attitude and confession must be positive at all times. If we find our confession getting weak, then we must immediately look to the Word of God for new strength and inspiration. We must discipline ourselves in this matter. We must dismiss every negative thought and doubt.

When questioned about our health we can say: 'I am trusting my divine Physician with all my heart. With His stripes He is making me well.' Each positive confession will bring you another wave of heaven-sent strength and health from the Lord Jesus. Make your lips and heart speak words of faith, and the Lord will reward and honour your confidence in Him. The scripture says, *'He will watch over His word in your heart and on your lips, to perform it.'* The full realisation of our healing may take a while, maybe not today, or tomorrow, but God's Word declares we will be healed and delivered. And so we must stand immovable upon the sure promises of the Lord. Memorise these promises, confess them from your heart and mouth, and then act upon them. Refuse to give in, always be positive and honour the word of the Lord.

The next point I want to emphasize is this. At all times we must see by faith our sicknesses and diseases upon the Lord Jesus Christ. We must recognise that sickness is part of His atoning work. The stripes of Jesus verify and justify our claim to divine healing at all times.

Continue to trust and believe, knowing delays are not denials. I knew a lady who was anointed and prayed for but nothing happened. For ninety-two days she gave thanks to God for her healing by faith. Then one day her goiter began to wither away until it completely disappeared. The Syrian General Naaman dipped seven times in the River Jordan before he was completely cured of leprosy. At first he argued and reasoned with God as to how he should receive his healing, but eventually he relented and obeyed the word of the Lord. He was not healed the first time he dipped in the Jordan, nor the second nor the third time. He washed seven times, refusing to be discouraged and giving glory to God. A blind man returned to Jesus for a second touch and only then was he fully cured. The walls of Jericho did not fall the first day the Israelites marched around them. For seven days they marched in silence and then on the seventh day gave a mighty shout and the walls came tumbling down. Their patience and persistence was well rewarded. Likewise we must refuse to be discouraged. In fact our situation may even deteriorate for a time because we have a strong enemy who will try to discourage us.

Charles Hadfield became blind as a teenager. He yielded his young life to Christ in one of my crusade services. The first time I prayed for his healing nothing happened. I prayed a second time but again nothing happened. He came again and Charles was gradually healed until his sight was fully restored. Today he can drive his own car and see to read and study without spectacles. Matty Evans was miraculously healed of a throat cancer during our West Wales visitation. The first service she attended nothing happened and she went home completely discouraged. However, faithful friends encouraged her to attend a second time. In that second service everything happened. Matty was wonderfully saved and miraculously healed by the power of God. Twelve years later she is still fit and well, giving glory to the Lord. So we must press through patiently expecting God's answer from heaven.

The next important issue concerns our faith. The Bible says that *'faith without works is dead'* (James 2:26). Many may sit around waiting for a miracle when maybe God is waiting for us to step out in faith upon His word. When the Master healed the sick He often gave a command of faith, *'rise, take up your bed and walk'*, *'go, show yourself to the priest'*, *'go to the pool of Siloam and wash.'* When the sufferers implicitly obeyed the Lord and acted in faith Jesus healed them. Our faith becomes a living force as we act upon the word of God. Once we have received the Lord's blessing and anointing it is time to act in faith. Of course, we must act sensibly and wisely, accomplishing all we do in the strength of Jesus' name. Each sufferer may begin to do the little tasks which proved impossible before.

I recall an incident which clearly defined the need for both faith and works. A boatman was rowing his friend across a lake. First he picked up one oar and began rowing fast and strong only to discover that he went round in a circle to the left. Placing that oar at the side of the boat saying 'that one doesn't work!' he picked up the other oar and began rowing fast and strong again only to find he went round in a circle in the right direction. Then he took up both oars and discovered by using both oars together he could go in a straight line and reach the other side. It is alright receiving our blessing and anointing, that is the first oar. But we must also use our second oar and put our faith into operation and act upon the Word of God. We must believe that the Lord is working with us and act accordingly. We must couple works with faith, for faith without works is dead.

Again we must act sensibly and with responsibility. I knew a lady who was wonderfully healed of arthritis but she began doing stupid things. She got a ladder and started painting the ceiling in her home. The ladder suddenly slipped and she fell hurting herself, and the arthritis returned through the shock. If she had acted sensibly her testimony would have remained intact. So we must be wise as we step out in faith.

I am questioned by those who are blessed in my healing services 'Should I give up my tablets and drugs after I've been prayed for?' This is a very sensitive issue and depends generally upon the individual concerned. I have known folk who have immediately discarded their drugs and have been miraculously cured. I have known others who have suffered excessively because they have ceased taking their prescribed dosage. It is essential to consult the Lord in prayer before taking any step in this direction. If we are fully assured by the Word of God then we may act accordingly. Even then we may seek the counsel of a Christian doctor or GP especially if we have been 'on drugs' during a prolonged period. Always remember it is our testimony that must be safeguarded. We must always do that which pleases the Lord. So prayerfully consider any step in this direction and the Lord will show you clearly what is best for you and for His Glory.

Chapter 18

Believing Is Receiving

I have received a number of letters from desperate Christians who have subscribed to the scriptural conditions of Divine Healing but have failed to receive benefit. Having considered these cases independently I have come across an aspect of faith which many overlook, i.e. **Believing is Receiving**. And before I can adequately share this important truth let us first reflect on three issues previously mentioned.

First, there is distinct difference between a healing and a miracle. A **miracle** is a decisive act of the sovereign will and power of God. The Lord appoints the time and place for a miracle. We may expect a miracle but cannot presume God for a miracle. Divine Healing, however, is an atonement provision for all true believers. (Matthew 8:17; 1 Peter 2:24).

Healing means 'to recover', suggesting a process rather than an instant work of grace.

Secondly, faith and hope are different virtues. Faith operates in the **present**, while hope contemplates the **future**.

Thirdly, divine healing is an ever-flowing stream of grace and blessing similar to forgiveness. Obey the

Lord, remove the hindrances and step into the stream to be healed.

Retain these important thoughts and now meditate upon 'Believing is Receiving'. Believing is always **in the now**. To think in terms of 'God **will** heal me' is hope. The moment you think of healing in the future is to move out of the realm of faith into hope. Some say: 'I **know** I will receive my healing' – that is hope, not faith; 'I will be healed at the time' – that is hope, not faith; 'I will be healed at the next healing service' – that is hope, not faith.

To **look forward** to receiving healing is to **hope, not to believe**. Faith is believing God is healing you **in the now – i.e. this present moment of time**.

True believing is already in the process of receiving. The moment you believe you activate the healing blessing of God. The moment you believe you step into the healing stream of His grace and power. The moment you believe, **you are being healed**. Believing is Receiving. Receiving is Believing.

When I lay my hands on the sick in the name of Jesus, I believe from that moment the sick person **is being healed**. The divine healing process begins at that very moment. God must honour His Word and He does. From that initial point of contact the healing grace of God begins to function. The sick person must recognise this without wavering. Whatever symptoms linger the sick one must accept that God is honouring His Word and Divine Healing has begun. And furthermore it is most important that this receiving attitude is maintained, so the healing grace of God can flow without restriction. The reason for the point of contact – e.g. the laying on of hands – is to initially release the flow of the Lord's healing grace. This should be accepted and appreciated by the sick one.

From that moment that person's attitude should be:

> 'God **is** healing me. The work **has** begun – and I will obey and give thanks to the Lord without wavering until it is complete.'

This positive attitude involves continuing communion and fellowship with Jesus. A constant consciousness of receiving the uninterrupted inflow of His healing grace and strength, always aware of continually bathing in the stream of Christ's healing love. While this attitude of receiving is maintained the healing is taking place.

I visited a young man in hospital. He was desperately ill with cancer. As I read a portion of Scripture tears filled his eyes. He was willing to yield his life to Christ and asked Jesus to save him. As I laid my hands upon him for Divine Healing I said,

'The Lord will begin healing you from this moment. The work will begin now! Accept this with all your heart. Jesus is healing you **now**! When I touched you His healing grace began flowing through your being. You are now beginning to recover. Do not be discouraged if the symptoms linger for a while. It will take a time. Be patient with the Lord. Maintain regular contact and communion with Jesus. It may help you to take up your Bible and imagine you are touching the hem of the Master's garment. Do this regularly. As you recover continue to give thanks and be determined to please and glorify God. Do not waver! Resist any doubt! The Lord has started a mighty work in your body and soul and He will perfect it. God is at work in you **now**! Keep receiving

It is to be appreciated that within the limited contents of this study there may be some issues still unresolved in the mind of the reader. Peter Scothern would welcome genuine enquiries relative to the Divine Healing ministry, prayer requests and blessed prayer handkerchiefs (Acts 19:11–12).

Please write to:

> Peter Scothern Ministries
> 150 Chatsworth Drive
> Mansfield
> Notts NG18 4QX
> United Kingdom
>
> (postage appreciated)

Website:
> www.peterscothernministries.com

– moment by moment – and let the glory and power of Jesus heal your body.'

The young man carried out those instructions to the letter and a few weeks later he was able to cycle to his place of employment. God is faithful. If you are sick, put your complete trust in the Lord and receive His healing grace **right now**!